The High-Performance Board

Dennis D. Pointer
James E. Orlikoff

The High-Performance Board

Principles of Nonprofit Organization Governance

JOSSEY-BASS
A Wiley Company
www.josseybass.com

Jossey-Bass books and products are available through most bookstores. To contact Jossey-Bass directly, call (888) 378-2537, fax to (800) 605-2665, or visit our website at www.josseybass.com.

Substantial discounts on bulk quantities of Jossey-Bass books are available to corporations, professional associations, and other organizations. For details and discount information, contact the special sales department at Jossey-Bass.

We at Jossey-Bass strive to use the most environmentally sensitive paper stocks available to us. Our publications are printed on acid-free recycled stock whenever possible, and our paper always meets or exceeds minimum GPO and EPA requirements.

Jossey-Bass also publishes its books in a variety of electronic formats. Some content that appears in print may not be available in electronic books.

Library of Congress Cataloging-in-Publication Data

Pointer, Dennis Dale.
  The high-performance board: principles of nonprofit
organization governance/Dennis D. Pointer, James E. Orlikoff.—
1st ed.
    p. cm.—(The Jossey-Bass nonprofit and public
management series)
Includes index.
  ISBN 0-7879-5697-X
  1. Nonprofit organizations—Management. 2. Boards of
directors. I. Orlikoff, James E. II. Title. III. Series.
HD62.6 .P66 2002
658.4'22—dc21

2002001090

HB Printing   10 9 8 7 6 5 4 3 2 1   FIRST EDITION

The Jossey-Bass
Nonprofit and Public Management Series

Contents

Figures and Check-Ups

Figures

Check-Ups

Preface

Governance is important work. How — and how well — it's done has significant consequences for nonprofit organizations, their clients, and the communities they serve.

Over the last twenty years we have served on numerous boards, consulted with thousands of boards, conducted research on boards, and written scores of books and articles about boards. We have profound respect for the significant contributions they make. The vast majority of nonprofit organization board members are talented and committed individuals who devote large amounts of time and effort to their roles.

Yet the performance and contributions of most boards are far from optimal.

We will have far more to say about this in Chapter One and throughout this book, but the reason is simple: very few boards base their governance on a set of explicit, precise, and coherent principles. In this book, we provide such principles, drawn from the vast literature in addition to our own consulting work with boards over the past twenty years.

A tremendous amount is known about the process of governing and what boards can do to dramatically improve their effectiveness, efficiency, and creativity in ways that enhance organizational success. And this knowledge, when employed, really does work. Here is one example from the commercial sector:

CalPERS, The California Public Employees Retirement System, is one of the largest pension funds in the country. In 1995–1996 it asked three hundred companies in its equity portfolio to consider adopting formal governance principles. CalPERS staff issued report cards and formulated and distributed a set of model—that is, benchmark—principles. (If you would like to see the latest version, log on to their Web site at http://www.calpers-governance.org.) A Wilshire Associates study of the "CalPERS effect" examined the performance of sixty-two companies over a ten-year period. Results indicated that whereas the stock of these companies trailed the Standard & Poors 500 Index by 89 percent in the five-year period before implementing CalPERS governance principles, the same stocks outperformed the Index by 23 percent in the five years after they were adopted, contributing approximately $150 million in additional returns to the Fund annually.

It is estimated that about half of the nation's largest commercial enterprises have adopted formal governance principles in some form (*Trustee Magazine*, July/August, 1998). Yet this is not common practice in the nonprofit sector.

Who Should Read This Book

This book is written from a point of view and has an agenda. Because we believe "principle-based governance" can significantly enhance board performance and contributions—and organizational success—our objective is to stimulate and facilitate the adoption of this approach in nonprofit organizations. The book is targeted at board members and executives who are committed to improving governance practice. This is not "governance-lite," it is a serious book for serious people who are willing to make a significant investment in their board's and organization's future.

What This Book Offers

This is a practical, how-to book. It provides

- A *model of governance*, which serves as the framework for Chapters Three through Seven

- *Sixty-four principles of high-performance governance* (and associated practices) for improving your board's performance and contributions

- *Getting started recommendations* to help your board begin adopting the principles

- *Check-ups* for assessing the extent your board presently employs the principles of benchmark governance

- *Guidelines* for transforming your board and implementing principle-based governance

---

Uses of This Book

- A comprehensive overview of nonprofit organization governance for newly appointed board members

- A "best practice" refresher for experienced board members

- An exemplar of what a truly great board looks like

- A blueprint for transforming your board . . . designing and implementing specific principles of governing that will dramatically improve its performance and contributions

- A template and set of specific criteria for rigorously assessing the quality of your board's governance quality

---

Charles Darwin presented a novel notion: in challenging environments where resources are scarce, if an organism has even a tiny edge over others, this advantage is amplified over time. He noted, in *Origin of the Species*, that a few grains of sand in the balance determine who thrives and who dies. Principle-based governance can tip a nonprofit organization's balance toward success.

This book provides an explicit, comprehensive, and coherent set of governance principles. The most basic principle is that the high-performance board appreciates the importance of governance and takes its work seriously. It devotes the necessary time and effort to governing, and it governs on the basis of agreed-to and explicit principles.

The high-performance board meets its fiduciary obligations by identifying key stakeholders and understanding their needs and expectations. It constantly represents, advances, and protects stakeholder interests, deciding and acting on their behalf, and ensuring that the organization's resources and capacities are deployed in ways that benefit them.

The high-performance board fulfills its responsibility for organizational ends (destination) by formulating a precise, detailed vision of what the organization should become — at its very best — in the future. It also specifies key goals that must be accomplished for the vision to be fulfilled, and makes sure that management develops strategies that are aligned with goals and the vision.

The high-performance board fulfills its responsibility for executive performance by specifying the CEO as its only direct report. It plans for CEO succession, undertaking an effective recruitment and selection process when the position of CEO becomes vacant. It specifies its expectations of the CEO and assesses the CEO's performance annually, providing feedback to improve that performance. It adjusts the CEO's compensation based on performance review results, and it is prepared to terminate the CEO's employment, should the need arise.

The high-performance board fulfills its responsibility for quality by recognizing that product and service quality and client satisfaction are essential to the organization's success. It develops an explicit and precise working definition of quality and then specifies a set of quality indicators and associated standards. With those standards in hand, it reviews management plans for managing and continuously improving both quality and client satisfaction.

The high-performance board fulfills its responsibility for finances by formulating key financial objectives, ensuring that management develops budgets that lead to accomplishing financial objectives, and specifying a set of financial indicators and associated standards. It also ensures that necessary financial controls are in place.

The high-performance board performs its core roles by formulating policies regarding its responsibilities that convey its expectations and directives. It makes decisions regarding matters requiring its attention and input, and it oversees (that is, monitors and assesses) key organizational processes and outcomes.

The high-performance board has an appropriate structure. It is right-sized, having between nine and nineteen members unless there is a compelling reason for a smaller or larger group. Where the organization has multiple boards, it explicitly specifies each board's authority, responsibilities, and roles. It has the right number and type of committees to support and facilitate its work—and it precisely specifies its authority vis-à-vis those committees, so that the board governs and committees perform governance staff work. It specifies the objectives, functions, and tasks of its committees, requiring them to develop annual work plans. It also reviews the need for, and functions of, all committees each year, and periodically assesses the overall governance structure and modifies it if necessary.

The high-performance board has the right composition. It proactively designs and manages its own composition, recruits and selects new members on the basis of explicit criteria, and has an effective new member orientation process. It specifies expectations of members and ensures that members do not represent narrow interests or constituencies. It has fixed member term lengths and limits. It assesses the performance and contributions of individual members. It includes the CEO as a voting member of the board, but ensures that *ex officio* and inside members hold no more than 25 percent of the board's seats.

The high-performance board has the necessary infrastructure in place. It has an annual governance budget and adequate staff support. It formulates annual governance objectives, employs a formal agenda planning and management process, and ensures board meetings are conducted in a way that optimizes their effectiveness, efficiency, and creativity. It makes sure that the presiding member is carefully selected and understands the role of the chair — and performs it effectively. It has a plan to continually develop board competencies and capacities, holds annual or semiannual retreats, and periodically assesses board performance and contributions, employing the results to engage in action planning that improves governance quality.

Before fully developing these principles, it's useful to consider several important caveats:

• Nonprofit organizations and their boards are an extremely diverse lot. Some are very large — national in scope, with resources in the billions that rival those of Fortune 500 companies, and with huge staffs. Wearing tailored suits, their members convene in specially designated board rooms and sit in leather chairs around walnut tables. Others are small — they serve locally focused organizations with tiny budgets and have little (and in many instances, no) staff support. The board arrives wearing jeans and sweatshirts, and meetings are held in a staff office or member's home. Such differences are simultaneously both superficial and consequential.

• All nonprofit boards have identical obligations (addressed in Chapter Two) and must do the same type of work to meet them (described in Chapters Three and Four). They must appropriately configure their "anatomy" and "physiology" (the topic of Chapters Five through Seven) to perform this work effectively, efficiently, and creatively. Accordingly, there are a set of generic principles of governing that transcend an organization's characteristics, circumstance, and situation.

• Nonetheless, governance context — particularly an organization's size — matters. Some of the principles are clearly not applicable to some boards. For example, many very small nonprofit organizations may not have management staff. Accordingly, principles 13 through 20 in Chapter Three will not be relevant to them. Other principles might be either impractical or difficult to fully implement. For example, principles 43 and 44 deal with committees, and some boards don't have or need them (yet the tasks described must be performed by members meeting as a whole). Likewise, principle 63 deals with board retreats, and an organization that lacks the resources to hold a retreat won't make use of the principle.

Rather than engaging in lengthy and cumbersome qualification of each principle, we rely on each reader to assess which are applicable to his or her specific board and which are not. Principles are general guidelines that must be tailored to specific circumstances, employing situational knowledge and judgment. We will provide principles, you supply the knowledge of your organization's and board's situation and liberal doses of judgment.

• Additionally, when it comes to mounting governance improvement initiatives, large organizations can deploy more resources. They can assign staff and hire consultants to aid and abet the process in ways that dwarf those available in smaller and less well-endowed organizations. As a consequence, the board of a small, resource-strapped nonprofit organization will have to go slower, target change efforts at implementing a narrower range of principles, and rely totally on internal capacities in doing so.

Reading this book, you may well feel overwhelmed by all the things your board can and should do to improve its performance and contributions. Don't be! This approach to governance improvement can produce significant results when focused on implementing a limited set of principles; a full court press is ideal but not necessary. This is a map for an entire journey that you might want to take. Begin with the first steps, have modest initial goals, don't obsess on what's left to be done, and celebrate wins as they come. Just keep at it and enjoy the trip.

The High-Performance Board is the product of what we have learned over the years from our fellow board members, clients, and consultant colleagues. They have been our teachers, and we are indebted to them. We dedicate this book to nonprofit organization board members; servant leaders and volunteers who make tremendous contributions to our society's well-being.

March 2002

Dennis D. Pointer
Dennis D. Pointer & Associates
509 Midway Street
La Jolla, CA 92037
206-499-1289
www.benchmarkgovernance.com

James E. Orlikoff
Orlikoff and Associates, Inc.
4800 S. Chicago Beach Drive,
   Suite 307N
Chicago, IL 60615-2054
773-268-8009
www.americangovernance.com

About the Authors

Dennis Pointer and James Orlikoff are among the nation's most highly regarded governance consultants, speakers, researchers, and writers. They collaborated on *Board Work*, published by Jossey-Bass in 1999, winner of the James A. Hamilton Book of the Year Award from the American College of Healthcare Executives.

Dennis D. Pointer has worked with over 400 clients. His firm, Dennis D. Pointer & Associates, provides governance consulting, retreat facilitation, assessment, redesign, and development services to nonprofit organizations, commercial corporations, and government agencies. He is also vice president of American Governance and Leadership Group LLC. The author of five other books and over seventy articles, Dr. Pointer holds the John J. Hanlon Endowed Chair at San Diego State University. Prior to joining the SDSU faculty in 1991, he was the Arthur Graham Glasgow Distinguished Professor at the Medical College of Virginia. From 1975 to 1986 he was affiliated with the University of California, Los Angeles, where he served as associate director of the UCLA Medical Center and professor and chairman of the Department of Health Services Management, School of Public Health. While at UCLA, Dr. Pointer was a senior research fellow at the RAND Corporation. He is a visiting professor at the University of Washington School of Public Health and Community Medicine. He received his Ph.D. from the University of Iowa and B.Sc. from Iowa State University.

James E. (Jamie) Orlikoff is president of Orlikoff and Associates, Inc., a firm specializing in governance improvement and leadership development. He is also executive director of the American Governance and Leadership Group LLC, which provides educational conferences, on-site programs, and consulting services for boards, board members, and other leaders. Mr. Orlikoff is the national adviser on governance and leadership to the American Hospital Association and former director of the organization's Division of Hospital Governance. In these various capacities, Mr. Orlikoff has worked with over six hundred organizations to strengthen their governance effectiveness and efficiency. He is the author of ten books and over a hundred articles, and was the founding editor and publisher of the *Health Governance Report,* a bimonthly newsletter on leadership issues and trends for board members. Mr. Orlikoff received his M.A. from the University of Chicago and B.A. from Pitzer College in Claremont, California; he sits on the Pitzer College board.

1

Governance Basics

There are approximately 3.5 million boards in the United States. This may seem an unbelievable figure until one considers that most commercial corporations, nonprofit organizations, and government agencies have them.

This book focuses on nonprofit governance, although many of the principles presented here can be employed by boards in other sectors.

Are Nonprofit Organizations and Their Governance Really Different?

The answer is both yes and no. Here are just a few illustrations:

The purpose of nonprofit organizations is public benefit—but the terms *public* and *benefit* are defined in a wide variety of ways. As a consequence, nonprofits are granted special privileges; subjected to distinctive laws, regulations, and reporting requirements; and often exempted from certain taxes.

Commercial corporation boards must satisfy shareholders, all of whom want essentially the same thing: a return on their investment. Nonprofit boards must meet the expectations of diverse stakeholder groups, each of whom may have very different (and even conflicting) interests.

Nonprofit organization board members are volunteers who have no direct economic interest in the success of the organizations. They don't own stock and are typically not compensated for their service.

Yet, even given such differences, the fundamental obligation and work of all boards is essentially the same. This obligation is addressed in the next chapter.

Boards bear ultimate authority and accountability for an organization's affairs. They are responsible for everything an organization is, does, and becomes. *Governance* is an activity, an action word; it is what boards do. The essence of the verb *to govern* is being a steward and trustee of an organization's resources and capacities.

Governance is a team sport. Boards exercise collective influence; their members have no individual power. Boards exist only when they meet, that is, "between raps of the gavel." Members may disagree, they can (and should) debate and argue about issues, but if they are going to decide and act, they must do so together.

Yet governance is part-time and occasional work. Although organizations, management, and employees are permanent fixtures, boards are not. They convene for a short period of time, adjourn, and then weeks or months pass until they meet again. Their attention, time, and energy are limited and fragmented. Additionally, governance is a peripheral aspect of board members' lives. No matter how important the issue being addressed, it is pushed aside when the meeting ends.

The Principles Behind the Principles

First, governance really matters. A board has significant impact on an organization's success or the lack thereof. A negative illustrates the point. Consider this challenge: Your board is given fifteen minutes to make decisions that would cause the organization great harm. Could you do it? Most board members respond, "Absolutely, it would be easy and we could do it in half the time." Does governance matter? You bet it does; for better or worse!

Second, governance is becoming more difficult. Due to the nature and pace of change, increasing size and complexity of nonprofit organizations, and greater demands for accountability, the crossbar has been raised. More is being expected of boards. In the past, appointment to a nonprofit organization board was first and foremost an honor. While this is still the case, stakeholders and clients are demanding much higher levels of performance and contributions.

Third, governance is less than optimal in most organizations. Recognizing their importance and how great they can be, we are tough on boards. The unavoidable fact is that many function far below their potential.

Fourth, board performance and contributions can be dramatically improved. Boards can make much more of a difference and add far greater value to their organizations than they do now. We have seen it happen. We've helped boards make it happen. But it doesn't just happen. Improving governance quality requires a number of factors:

- Dissatisfaction with the status quo. Boards pleased with their present level of performance don't change, as they see no need to do so.

- An image of what governance should be like at its very best.

- Significant time and energy devoted to undertaking development initiatives that must be added to that already spent governing.

- Follow through. Major change always creates back pressure for gradually returning to the far more comfortable way things were done in the past.

A transformation in how nonprofit organization boards govern must be based on specific principles that promote best practice.

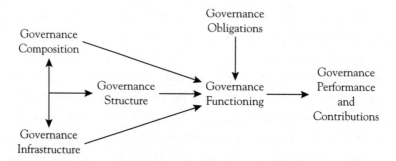

Figure 1.1. Key Determinants of Governance Quality.

This book presents sixty-four such principles based on a model (presented in Figure 1.1) of factors that most affect board performance and contributions. (The principles are presented in each chapter, as they become relevant to the discussion. For a look at the whole list, see Resource A at the end of the book.)

- *Obligations:* the purpose of boards and value they add

- *Functioning:* how boards define and do their work (fulfilling responsibilities and performing roles)

- *Structure:* the way governance work is subdivided, shared, and coordinated

- *Composition:* board member characteristics, knowledge, skills, experience, perspectives, and values

- *Infrastructure:* resources and systems that facilitate and support the board and its work

Clearly, a host of factors affect governance quality. But these are the ones we have found to matter most. This prompts our first principle:

Principle 1

The board realizes that it alone bears ultimate responsibility, authority, and accountability for the organization. It understands the importance of governance and undertakes its work with a sense of seriousness and purpose.

Your board has no capacity for doing the organization's real work: producing products and services that meet client needs. Additionally, it cannot manage the organization and should not attempt to do so. Yet it is ultimately responsible for both. Your board is, to quote Harry Truman, the place where "the buck stops."

Your board must fully appreciate its obligations before it can fulfill them. Recognizing the importance of governance is a prerequisite for doing it well. Few people are willing to devote large amounts of time and effort to activities they deem insignificant.

We've worked with boards whose members believe governance is trivial, relatively inconsequential to the organization's success. We have worked with boards where members are either unable or unwilling to devote the necessary time and energy to governing. In such cases, little can be done to improve governance; the motivation and energy does not exist.

Principle 2

The board understands those factors that most affect governance quality and employs a coherent set of principles to govern.

Many boards practice idiosyncratic governance based largely on personal experience, situational logic, and habit. While this may result in acceptable and even occasionally good governance, it is an inherently limiting approach. Optimal performance and contributions are grounded on principles specifying board obligations, functions, structure, composition, and infrastructure.

1. My board appreciates the importance   low   medium   high
   of governance to the organization,   1   2   3
   and takes its work seriously.

2. My board understands those factors   low   medium   high
   that most affect its performance   1   2   3
   and contributions.

3. Members of my board devote the   low   medium   high
   necessary time and effort to governing.   1   2   3

4. My board governs on the basis of   low   medium   high
   an agreed-upon set of principles.   1   2   3

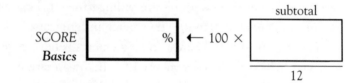

$$\text{SCORE Basics} \boxed{ \%} \leftarrow 100 \times \frac{\boxed{\text{subtotal}}}{12}$$

Check-Up 1.1. Basics.

Scoring: Respond to all items. Total your responses for the four items, divide by 12, and then multiply by 100. The product is your board's percentage of maximum performance in this area.

Throughout the book, a series of check-ups will give you the opportunity to assess your board in light of benchmark governance principles. In Chapter Eight the individual check-ups will be combined to produce a governance performance profile.

When completing these check-ups, be descriptive and discriminating. Portray your board's actual characteristics and practices. Be honest and candid; don't fall victim to the "halo effect" and rate everything high because you admire your board. All boards excel in some areas and are poor in others, and your responses should reflect this.

Getting Started: Basics

- Continually reinforce the importance of the board and governance work to the organization—during the orientation of new members, through educational activities, at meetings, before critical issues are addressed.

- Remember that people recognize work as important when it is appreciated. Seize every opportunity to acknowledge and celebrate your board's accomplishments and efforts.

- Begin crafting a set of principles for your board: simple declarative statements that specify how your board will govern.

- Employ the "getting started" recommendations provided throughout the book to formulate the initial elements of a continuous improvement action plan for your board.

2

Obligations

This chapter deals with the most foundational governance question: Why do nonprofit organizations need boards?

From a legal perspective, the answer is because they must have them. State laws of incorporation require them. From a functional perspective the answer is less straightforward and more complex: to represent the interests of stakeholders and make sure the organization benefits them.

Your board has the potential to add considerable value. But the key term is *potential*, which can only be realized if your board understands and fulfills its obligations.

Principle 3

The overarching obligation of a board is ensuring an organization's resources and capacities are deployed in ways that benefit its stakeholders. The board serves as their agent, representing, protecting, and advancing their interests and acting on their behalf.

This principle goes to the very heart of your board's fundamental purpose.

All organizations are created and maintained to benefit someone. The question is: Who? The answer varies:

- Commercial corporations are formed to benefit *shareholders*, that is, the individuals and groups who own their stock.

- Nonprofit organizations are created to benefit *stakeholders*, groups that are the equivalent of a for-profit's owners. However, unlike shareholders, stakeholders are not actual owners; they do not have a claim on the organization's assets nor do they receive a share of its excess revenues.

- Government agencies are designed to benefit *constituents*, that is, voters, citizens, or some segment of the population.

Organizations: For Whose Benefit?

Some contend that organizations are created to benefit customers. If you own stock in a commercial corporation, it's unlikely that you'd accept this argument. An organization's ultimate purpose is to benefit those who have invested in it, stockholders; it does so by meeting the needs of customers. Stockholder benefit is the *end,* customer satisfaction is the *means.* The same is true in nonprofits. Stakeholders are the owners whose interests the organization must protect and advance. Nonprofits do this by serving their clients. What makes things complex is that for many nonprofits, stakeholders and clients are often the same. For example: the owners of a mutual insurance company or a co-op are also its clients; the patients of a nonprofit hospital are typically considered stakeholders; the stakeholders of a professional or trade association are also its members. While this confuses matters, the principle still holds: nonprofit organizations are created and maintained to benefit stakeholders. It is a board's ultimate obligation to see this is the case.

When asked "What is your board's most fundamental and important obligation?" most members will reply, "We're here to ensure the organization survives and thrives." This answer is off the mark and provides an inappropriate starting point for great (or even good) governance.

Means and Ends

Nonprofit organizations are collections of resources: money, people, facilities, equipment, and supplies; they are means. And their end is benefiting stakeholders.

Your board's overarching obligation is representing, advancing, and protecting stakeholder interests: deciding and acting on their behalf, serving as their agent. This is the bedrock of governance. High-performance governance begins with a clear, precise, and shared notion of *why*, and for what purpose, your board exists. Only with clarity and consensus here can your board determine *what* it must do and *how* it should go about doing it.

Principle 4

The board identifies the organization's key stakeholders.

Once your board understands its overarching obligation to stakeholders, it must identify them explicitly and precisely.

Stakeholders: Who the Heck Are They?

An easy question to answer, you say? Typically, not the case in most nonprofits.

When addressing this topic at retreats we ask board members to take out a piece of paper and list who they think their organization's most important stakeholders are—those whose interests the board should represent. Invariably, the responses we get are all over the lot; there is not much agreement. Give this a try at your next board meeting.

How can your board fulfill its obligation to govern on behalf of stakeholders if members either don't know, or disagree among themselves, about who they are? The answer is, of course, it can't.

It is here that nonprofit organizations differ significantly from commercial corporations. The owners of commercial corporations are easily identified: everyone who owns stock.

Things are not so simple for nonprofits. Granted, a charter or articles of incorporation typically denote who the organization was initially formed to benefit. However, the wording is usually vague. Terms such as *citizens, community, the public, patrons, clients, members,* or *the common good* are the norm. Additionally, designations developed in the past may not be relevant today.

So, who are they? Here are illustrative stakeholders for several different types of nonprofit organizations:

A private college	• students
	• parents of students
	• faculty
	• major donors
	• the largest research funders
	• alumni
A church	• sponsoring religious community
	• members of the congregation not included in other categories
	• large givers
	• those who volunteer significant amounts of time

A professional association	• members who are specialty practitioners
	• members who are general practitioners
	• licensing bodies
A Catholic hospital	• the sponsoring religious congregation
	• actual and potential patients
	• the poor and uninsured residing in the primary service area
	• members of the medical staff
A symphony orchestra	• corporate patrons
	• individual patrons
	• season ticket holders
	• regular event attendees
	• orchestra members

Employing guidance provided by the charter, articles of incorporation, precedents from earlier board action, and the organization's own history, your board must identify its stakeholders: those whom the organization is designed to benefit; those whose interests your board must represent.

We have helped many boards conduct stakeholder analyses. Among the most important things we have learned is that it isn't necessary or even desirable to specify every conceivable stakeholder, just the most important ones.

The initial process need not be perfect; you can begin and then refine selections over time. It's best to keep the list short—in most cases under a half-dozen.

Be specific. Craft a description of each group of stakeholders and describe their most important characteristics. Formulate a brief rationale stating why each should be treated as an organizational owner.

Subdivide stakeholder groups by their differing interests. For example, at first glance the board of an apartment homeowners' association might identify only one stakeholder group: those who own apartments in the complex. However, different types of owners (for example, those who reside in their apartments and those who maintain them as rental properties) have different interests; here, there are several stakeholders, not just one.

Recognize that this is hard intellectual work, fraught with tough choices, traps, and blind alleys. Striving for precision regarding who the organization's stakeholders are, or should be, will generate some conflict. And although stakeholders are typically stable over time, they can and do change. Thus, your board should periodically review its listing.

Principle 5

The board understands stakeholder interests and expectations.

Once your board has identified stakeholders, it must understand their interests—what they want from and expect of the organization. Specificity is the key; vague generalities are of little value. Your board must be able to answer the following questions:

- To what extent, and how, is each stakeholder group dependent upon the organization? And how (and in what way) is the organization's success dependent on each?

- What does each stakeholder group expect the organization to accomplish on its behalf?

- From each stakeholder's perspective, how is the organization's success defined?

- How well does the organization meet the expectations and fulfill the needs of each stakeholder? What specific things must the organization do to better further their interests?

Illustrative Stakeholder Interests and Expectations: Sponsoring Religious Community of a Catholic Hospital

- We expect the Hospital's clinical programs to conform with the Catholic Church's clinical ethical directives.
- We expect the Hospital's vision, key goals, and strategies to manifest the guiding principles of the Sisters of St. ____.
- We expect the Hospital to achieve a net margin from operations of at least X.X percent.
- We expect that no less than XX percent of total net margin from operations will be employed to provide care to the poor, disadvantaged, and underserved residing in the Hospital's primary service area or made available to the _____ Community Benefit Trust.

A dossier should be prepared on each stakeholder group and updated periodically, describing them and noting their most significant interests and expectations.

Principle 6

The board decides and acts on behalf of stakeholders; it discharges its legal fiduciary duty of loyalty.

Identifying stakeholders and understanding their interests is the foundation of high-performance governance. Deliberating and deciding on their behalf in a manner that protects and advances these interests is the most fundamental governance practice.

Statutory and case law hold that boards owe allegiance to their organization's stakeholders, acting in their best interests rather than for personal gain or for the benefit of other organizations, groups, or individuals. The dealings of boards must meet two tests. First, they must have good-faith intentions: a desire to serve stakeholders. Second, they must behave in ways that demonstrate their decisions are made to further the interests of stakeholders.

Board members breach their duty of loyalty when, for example, a material conflict of interest influences their decisions, when they seize an opportunity for themselves or other parties that legitimately belongs to the organization, or vote in favor of a distribution of the organization's assets that subverts its purposes, impairs advancing stakeholder interests, or results in private inurement.

Your board can make sure it is discharging its duty of loyalty by (as addressed in principles 4 and 5) identifying stakeholders and understanding their interests, and having a vision and mission statement that clearly and precisely specifies the organization's purposes and the nature of benefits provided to stakeholders. Your board's responsibility for envisioning the organization will be addressed in Chapter Three. The board also needs to have a policy that specifically defines material conflicts of interest and requires board members to acknowledge such conflicts when they arise (prior to participating in deliberations) in addition to refraining from discussing, influencing, or voting on matters where such a conflict exists. The board must constantly remind members of their duty of loyalty (and obligation to act in the best interest of stakeholders) prior to voting on major issues.

Principle 7

The board discharges its legal fiduciary duty of care.

Not only must your board be loyal to stakeholders, it must be careful in doing so. The law requires board members to take "due care" in discharging their responsibilities. They must be reasonable, diligent, and prudent, and demonstrate sound judgment equal to that of an ordinarily competent person in similar circumstances. The duty of care focuses on the process of deciding and acting, not the results. The test is: Was reasonable care exercised? Not: Were the results optimal, satisfactory, or even tolerable?

Your board is permitted to presume that information, analyses, and recommendations provided by others (such as management, staff, and consultants) are accurate, truthful, and informed if there is no compelling reason to believe otherwise. The courts are very hesitant to substitute their judgment, after the fact, for that of your board. The expectation is simply that members act carefully with common sense and reasonable, informed judgment.

This duty is most often breached by boards collectively, not by the actions or inaction of individual members. Problems typically arise regarding matters involving large expenditures, fundamental changes in mission, and disposition of the organization's assets.

Your board can ensure it is discharging its duty of care by having legal counsel recap your board's duty of care (in addition to loyalty) prior to deliberating and acting on major issues. It should also make sure that analyses undertaken by staff and consultants are thorough and accurately portray both the positives and negatives of a proposed initiative. Its procedures should include distributing background materials well before board meetings so members can carefully review and reflect upon key issues, and also allowing enough time at board meetings for full discussion, questions, elaboration and clarification, and deliberation and debate prior to votes on important matters. Before key votes, it is useful to conduct an informal audit and discuss whether your board has exercised its duty of care regarding the matter.

Principle 8

The board understands the functions it must perform in order to meet its obligations.

The single most important determinant of governance quality is how your board chooses to function. Peter Drucker defines effectiveness as "doing the right things." To be effective your board must

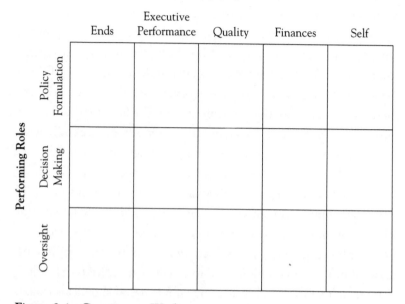

Figure 2.1. Governance Work.

Note: Governance work is a 3 × 5 matrix. To meet its obligations, a board must formulate policies about, decide, and oversee ends, executive performance, quality, finances, and its own activities.

have an explicit, precise, coherent, and shared definition of the things it should be doing, the key aspects of its work.

Governance work has two facets: fulfilling responsibilities and performing roles. *Responsibilities* are the "what" aspects of governance, the substantive issues and matters to which your board must attend. *Roles* are the "how" aspect, the sets of activities your board must perform. Together, responsibilities and roles specify the essence of the verb *to govern*, answering the question: What type of work should my board be doing?

Your board has five responsibilities, as sketched in Figure 2.1:

• Formulating the organization's *ends*, its vision, and key goals in addition to ensuring strategies are aligned with the vision and goals

- Ensuring high levels of *executive performance*

- Ensuring the organization produces *high-quality* offerings that meet client needs

- Ensuring the organization's *financial* health

- Ensuring the board's own effectiveness, efficiency, and creativity—denoted as *self* in the figure

To fulfill these responsibilities, your board must perform three roles:

- *Policy formulation*, specifying its expectations and directives

- *Decision making*, choosing among alternatives regarding matters requiring board input

- *Oversight*, monitoring and assessing key aspects of organizational performance and outcomes

The types of things your board could do are virtually unlimited; statutory law and court decisions impose relatively few restrictions. However, boards are good at certain things and lousy at others. Additionally, board attention, time, and energy is severely limited. Thus, to focus and leverage its effort, your board must do the type of work that makes the most difference (on behalf of stakeholders) and adds the greatest value (to the organization): formulating policy, making decisions, and overseeing ends, executive performance, quality, finances, and its own activities.

Principles regarding your board's responsibility for ends, executive performance, quality, and finances are presented in Chapter Three. Chapter Four focuses on the roles of policy formulation, decision making, and oversight. Chapters Five through Seven address your board's responsibility for itself: its structure, composition, and infrastructure.

	low	medium	high
1. My board understands and fulfills its overarching obligation: representing, advancing, and protecting stakeholder interests.	1	2	3
2. My board has explicitly and precisely identified the organization's key stakeholders.	1	2	3
3. My board understands the expectations and interests of key stakeholder groups.	1	2	3
4. My board discharges its legal fiduciary duty of loyalty; we decide and act on behalf of stakeholders.	1	2	3
5. My board discharges its legal fiduciary duty of care; we act prudently, reasonably, and with informed judgment.	1	2	3
6. Members of my board have a precise, coherent, and shared understanding of the responsibilities we must fulfill and the roles we must perform in order to meet our obligations.	1	2	3

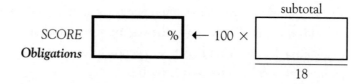

SCORE
Obligations
[   ] % ←— 100 × subtotal [   ] / 18

Check-Up 2.1. Obligations.

Scoring: Respond to all items. Total your responses for the six items, divide by 18, and then multiply by 100. The product is your board's percentage of maximum performance in this area.

Getting Started: Obligations

- Spend some time at an upcoming meeting discussing your board's fundamental obligation to represent the interests of stakeholders. What are the practical implications of this obligation? When, and how, has your board done this at its best? What are some instances where this obligation was not met? What were the consequences? What did your board learn from this? What should be changed as a result?

- If your board has never (or not recently) conducted a stakeholder analysis, do so. Start by identifying and developing an understanding of the interests and expectations of your organization's most important stakeholders. This deliberation should probably take place over a half-day at a retreat. Our suggestion is to start small and focus on less than a half-dozen stakeholders.

- When major issues and important matters are being discussed, encourage board members to take a stakeholder perspective. Reinforce obligations and the duties of loyalty and care. Board deliberations can often become diffused and confused when members argue their individual points of view. Realize that although members must be true to their values, they do not sit on the board to advance their own agendas; they are there to represent stakeholders.

3

Functioning
Responsibilities

This chapter focuses on half of what your board must do to function effectively: fulfill its responsibilities for ends, executive performance, quality, finances, and itself. This is the central aspect of governance, your board's biggest job and also the book's longest chapter.

The other half of governance functioning, performing roles, is addressed in Chapter Four.

ENDS
Principle 9

The board understands and accepts its ultimate responsibility for determining the organization's ends and ensuring it has a plan for achieving them.

An organization is a means for accomplishing ends. Determining which it will pursue — and which it won't — is your board's responsibility. To fulfill it your board must formulate the organization's vision, specify its key goals, and ensure that management strategies are likely to accomplish key goals and fulfill the vision.

The organization pursues ends on behalf of its stakeholders. Thus, if your board has not identified its stakeholders (principle 4) and does not understand their interests (principle 5), it cannot formulate meaningful ends on their behalf.

In specifying ends, your board defines the organization, now and in the future. Governance begins here; your board's other responsibilities (for management, quality, finances, and itself) all flow from this one.

Principle 10

The board formulates the organization's vision.

Mention *vision* and what pops into most people's mind is something like this:

> **The organization's vision is to become the best [organization of its type] and provide clients with the highest-quality services at the lowest possible costs.**

The notion we will be developing bears no resemblance to this type of vague and meaningless statement.

How Vision and Mission Differ

Visions imagine the future, pointing to where an organization should go. Missions define the present, describing what an organization is. Visions challenge, missions anchor.

Both are important, but we will focus on vision here. The reason: your organization cannot alter its mission, which has been determined by past decisions and actions. Formulating the vision is your board's best lever for influencing the organization's future on behalf of its stakeholders.

Although they may differ in a variety of other ways, successful organizations have one thing in common: they have precise, coherent, and empowering visions. The reason is simple; an organization cannot achieve that which is not envisioned.

A *vision* is a description of what the organization should and could become, at its very best. It spells the difference between purposefully moving or aimlessly wandering into the future. Visions are composed of core purposes and values.

Core purposes are the most important things an organization wants to achieve. Stating them answers the following questions:

- Why should the organization exist and what should it exist for?

- In what ways should it be different from what it is now?

- What should it not become? How should it remain the same?

- What must the organization do to advance the interests and meet the needs and expectations of key stakeholders?

- What type of clients should the organization serve? Who should it be serving that it is not? What types of clients should it avoid?

- What types of benefits, services, and products should the organization provide?

Core purposes are not listings of objectives (such as market share targets). Rather, they are your organization's reason for being in the future.

Core values are the most important things for which an organization should stand. To define them, answer the following questions:

- What are the ultimate principles that should guide the organization's decisions and actions?

- What "thou shalts" and "thou shalt nots" should the organization respect?

• What ultimate values should define the organization's
heart and soul? What words should it live by?

Core values comprise the organization's constitution; its most cherished and central truths.

An empowering and useful vision is specific, precise, and detailed — a graphic portrait, not an abstract painting, of what the organization should look like. It describes the organization at its best and is future oriented.

We want to emphasize a key point: your board must craft the organization's vision; this is not a responsibility that should be delegated to management. Management should not develop a vision statement for your board to review and then approve after superficial discussion and deliberation. While your board is responsible for formulating the vision, it requires assistance in doing so. Visioning must be based on careful and thorough analyses of the organization's market, clients, and competitors in addition to its own strengths and weaknesses; management does these analyses and presents them to the board.

Generating a vision is often inhibited by the attempt to produce an elegant statement. The emphasis becomes wordsmithing rather than substance. Accordingly, we recommend beginning by drafting bulleted lists of what your organization's purposes and values should be — probably not exceeding a dozen such statements. Don't try for perfection! Attempting to come up with the perfect vision statement will stall and eventually sabotage the effort to produce a good one. Get started, do something. Regard everything as a work in progress that can be refined over time.

Principle 11

The board specifies key organizational goals.

Visioning will amount to little absent the development of key goals. *Goals* are specific accomplishables — the most important things the organization must achieve to fulfill its vision. Key goals increase the richness and density of the organization's vision, saying: "Above all else, accomplish these things."

Your board should specify key organizational goals that are few in number. In most instances an organization needs no more than a dozen, focusing only on the most vision-critical things your board wants accomplished. The goals should be realistically achievable while stretching the organization's capacities, competencies, and potential. In addition, they should be

- *Quantifiable:* providing precise targets and clear measures of success, or lack thereof.

- *Time specific:* providing a clear indication of when they should be achieved. (Note that most key goals need not be annual, as the most important ones generally take years to accomplish.)

- *Consistent:* so that accomplishing one goal does not impair prospects for achieving others.

- *Brief, crisply worded, and unequivocal:* so there can be no confusion about what is expected.

The board should review the goals and if necessary modify them annually. Key goals should have a relatively long shelf-life, but if the situation and organizational challenges change, the goals should change accordingly.

Your board has an obligation to formulate and articulate the most important things it expects the organization to accomplish in order to fulfill its vision. Additionally, strategies (to which we turn next) cannot be developed unless key goals have been specified.

Principle 12

The board does not become directly involved in developing organizational strategies; it delegates this task to management.

Ask a board member, or an executive for that matter, whether a board ought to be involved in strategy formulation and the answer you get is: "Of course they should." Indeed, boards should be strategically focused—but that's not the same as developing strategy.

Strategies are plans for allocating an organization's resources in ways that accomplish goals. Whereas vision and key goals are your board's responsibility, developing strategy is management's. It demands time and expertise in addition to knowledge about the market, clients, competitors, and the organization's own capacities that exceeds that possessed by even the very best boards.

Should your board then wash its hands of all things strategic? No. Instead, each year, management should develop a set of core organization-wide strategies, each accompanied by a concise rationale stating how it is linked to accomplishing one or more board-formulated key goals and to fulfilling the vision. Your board then reviews these core strategies (and accompanying rationales), addressing the following questions: Is each strategy aligned with the vision and key goals? Is the rationale sound? Will the proposed strategy likely lead to accomplishing one or more key goals and contribute to the vision being fulfilled? If, for any reason, the answer is no, the strategy is referred back to management for modification or elimination.

This approach (where your board focuses on vision and goals and management focuses on strategy) effectively subdivides and coordinates governance and managerial responsibilities, reduces duplication of effort, and minimizes conflict.

Governance and Management Work

Governance and management are fundamentally different, but complimentary, organizational functions. Here is an overarching principle:

*A great board appreciates the difference between running
an organization and seeing it's well run. Management
is the former, governance is the latter.*

The single most important decision your board makes (and it's made over and over again) is where to draw the line between governance and management work. If the line is too high, your board abdicates its responsibility. On the other hand, if it is too low, your board becomes overwhelmed in detail, besides taking on tasks it is unable to do well.

The principles dealing with your board's obligations and responsibility for ends illustrate this key point. To optimize its effectiveness and leverage, your board should focus its very limited attention, time, and energy on identifying stakeholders and understanding their interests, formulating a vision, and specifying key goals. Boards have the collective perspective, competence, and wisdom to do these things. And doing them adds real value to the organization on behalf of stakeholders. Management should then focus on developing strategy. It has the time, expertise, and knowledge to do so, whereas the board does not.

---

1. My board appreciates the nature and importance of its responsibility for ends.

    low 1   medium 2   high 3

2. My board has formulated a detailed, precise, and empowering vision for the organization, specifying its core purposes and values.

    low 1   medium 2   high 3

3. My board has developed key organizational goals that must be accomplished to fulfill the vision.

    low 1   medium 2   high 3

4. My board does not develop strategies; rather, it assesses the extent to which

    low 1   medium 2   high 3

(*continued*)

> management strategies are aligned with key goals and the vision, and likely to achieve them.

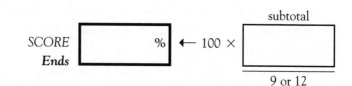

$$\begin{array}{c} SCORE \\ \textit{Ends} \end{array} \boxed{\qquad \%} \leftarrow 100 \times \boxed{\qquad}$$

subtotal

9 or 12

Check-Up 3.1. Ends.

Scoring: Respond to item 4 only if your organization has a CEO. Total your responses for the items you answer, divide by either 9 or 12 (the number of items times 3), and then multiply by 100. The product is your board's percentage of maximum performance in this area.

Getting Started: Ends

- Set aside some time at an upcoming board meeting and assess the organization's vision and key goals. How long has it been since they were seriously reworked? Has your board been proactively involved in formulating them? Or is this a task that has been delegated (either by design or default) to management? Does the vision crisply and clearly state core purposes and values? Is it a rich description of what the organization should look like at its very best in the future? Are goals truly key, the most vision-critical accomplishables? Are goals few in number, achievable, quantifiable, time specific, consistent, and brief?

- If the organization's vision and key goals don't pass muster, hold a half-day board retreat to brainstorm a short initial set of core purposes, core values, and key goals. They can be reworked by an ad hoc committee and then presented to your board for discussion, reworking, and approval.

MANAGEMENT
Principle 13

The board understands it is ultimately responsible for ensuring high levels of executive performance.

Your board's job is governing, not managing. Indeed, the more your board attempts to manage, the less it will be able to govern. The eventual losers are the organization and its stakeholders.

Yet your board is responsible and accountable for ensuring the organization is well managed. To fulfill this responsibility it must recruit and select the chief executive officer, the CEO. (Titles vary—you'll see administrator, director, executive director, and others—but CEO is the one we employ here for consistency's sake. This is the person who is directly accountable to the board for the organization's operations.) It must then specify its expectations of the CEO, assess the CEO's performance, and periodically adjust the CEO's compensation package. Should the need arise, it must be prepared to terminate the CEO's employment.

In fulfilling this responsibility, the overarching objective of your board should be focusing the CEO's attention and energy on fulfilling the vision and accomplishing key goals on behalf of stakeholders.

Principle 14

The CEO is the board's only direct report.

Your board should have only one direct report, the CEO; all other employees are accountable either directly or indirectly to the CEO, not the board. This creates a clear chain of command that minimizes mixed signals and conflict.

Several implications flow from this principle:

• Your board, and especially individual board members, should neither make requests of nor direct other management staff or employees.

- Recruiting and selecting other management staff and employees should be the responsibility of the CEO and those who report to the CEO.

- Your board should not become involved in assessing the performance or adjusting the compensation of managers and staff who report to the CEO.

Principle 15

When a vacancy occurs, the board selects the CEO.

When the position becomes vacant (and at some time in the future it will), recruiting and selecting a CEO is one of the most important tasks your board will ever undertake. The decision has a profound impact on your board and the organization's success. Top performers are hard to find, and the best people are generally not seeking new positions. Until a new CEO is recruited, the organization's operational metabolism slows down and key strategic issues are put on hold. Most board members who have been involved in a CEO search say it is the most time-consuming, stressful, and challenging aspect of governance work.

Recruiting a CEO requires special expertise, experience, time, and contacts that many boards do not possess. Therefore, if possible, we strongly recommend seeking some outside assistance. This could be provided by a search consultant retained by your board or help provided by a parent organization or trade association.

We have observed and participated in a number of executive searches. Here are a few success criteria:

- Appoint an ad hoc search committee composed only of board members; the executive committee could take on this task. The search committee should be chaired by the board chair. Key decisions (such as selecting the final candidate) should be made by the full board on the basis of the committee's work.

- Base recruitment, screening, and selection on a precise and explicit specification of the competencies and capacities needed to lead the organization into its future, fulfilling its vision and accomplishing key goals; the extent to which a candidate's values mesh with those of the organization; and personal characteristics deemed important by your board.

- The single best predictor of future success is past success; pay attention to the track records of candidates. Have they led other organizations down the path yours wants to travel?

Principle 16

The board has a CEO succession plan.

CEO departure (due to death, retirement, seeking other opportunities, or removal) is something that most boards don't like to think about or plan for. Often the response is: "We'll cross that bridge when we come to it." Vacancies in the top slot usually arise unexpectedly and seem to occur at the worst possible moment. When they do so, the board reacts with surprise rather than careful and thoughtful planning, which is costly and disruptive to the organization.

"Be prepared" is excellent advice. Your board should have a CEO succession plan in place that specifies who will assume the CEO's duties on an interim basis—and how present responsibilities of the interim CEO will be distributed among other management staff. (Failure is assured when someone attempts to hold down several jobs simultaneously.) The plan should also specify if and how the interim CEO's compensation will be temporarily adjusted to reflect additional responsibilities, and whether the interim CEO should be encouraged, discouraged, or prohibited from applying for the permanent position.

Principle 17

The board specifies its key expectations of the CEO.

As your board's only direct report, the CEO is accountable to it for carrying out its policies and decisions. Accordingly, your board must explicitly and precisely convey what it expects of and wants from the CEO. We continue to be amazed how few boards engage in this absolutely essential governance practice. The boxed text presents some illustrative expectations.

Illustrative CEO Expectations

- In all dealings on behalf of, and within, the organization acting in way that would be deemed as both legal and ethical.

- Keeping our board fully informed of all matters that might affect the organization's ability to fulfill its vision, accomplish its goals, and achieve its financial objectives.

- Over the next year, participate in at least forty hours of continuing professional education to improve your knowledge and skills in the areas of nonprofit organization managerial accounting and finance.

- Oversee the successful design and implementation of a "total client satisfaction" program (success criteria specified in board meeting minutes of XX/XX/XX).

- Facilitate and ensure the organization meets board-specified financial objectives.

- Within the next year, assume a leadership role in at least one key community group.

- Retain a chief operating officer by no later than XX/XX/XX; in addition to discharging the duties associated with the role, this individual should be capable of assuming the position of CEO on an interim basis should the need arise.

- Consummate an affiliation agreement with [group] prior to XX/XX/XX with favorable terms to our organization as approved by the board.

- Annually, make at least XX presentations to key stakeholder and community groups regarding the vision and mission of the organization.

Here are some guidelines:

- Specify only the most important expectations; the ones the CEO must fulfill to do a great job in the eyes of your board.

- Craft expectations that are operational and quantifiable, if possible. At the same time, do not avoid expressing critical expectations just because they can't be precisely measured.

- Focus on things over which the CEO has control.

- Involve the CEO in the process.

- Update and revise your board's expectation list annually.

- Codify your expectations. Reducing them to writing encourages precision.

Principle 18

Annually, employing explicit criteria, the board assesses the CEO's performance and contributions.

Board members continually evaluate a CEO's performance; it's unavoidable. The problem with most such evaluations, however, is that they are sporadic and idiosyncratic, focusing on isolated events and behaviors.

Designing and employing a formal periodic CEO performance assessment process is essential as it provides your board its best opportunity for better understanding the CEO's responsibilities and challenges; focusing the CEO's attention and energy on what really matters; clarifying mutual expectations; providing the CEO with feedback, direction, and affirmation; encouraging continuing professional development; and constructing the foundation upon which the CEO's compensation is adjusted.

Your board cannot undertake an assessment of the CEO unless the necessary prerequisites are in place: a fully fleshed out vision, clear and measurable organizational goals, precise strategies, and specific CEO performance expectations. The process must be designed to help your board answer two questions: Over the past year, to what extent has the CEO contributed to fulfilling the organization's vision (principle 10), accomplishing its key goals (principle 11), pursuing its strategies effectively (principle 12), and meeting its financial objectives (to be addressed in principle 26)? To what extent did the CEO meet the board's performance expectations (principle 17)?

We suggest the following:

- In line with principle 14, your board should assess only the CEO's performance.

- While a committee might do the groundwork, the full board should thoroughly discuss and approve the completed evaluation.

- The CEO should be a partner in the process, not just an object of it, and should have a voice in developing assessment criteria.

- The CEO should undertake an assessment of his or her own performance, which should then be used as one input by your board in doing its evaluation.

- Your board must provide the CEO with explicit and candid feedback and work with the CEO to develop action plans to continually improve performance.

Principle 19

Annually, the board adjusts the CEO's compensation.

Appraisal of the CEO's performance provides the basis for compensation adjustments. Technique, method, tax considerations, and legalities can be overwhelming. Accordingly, this is an area where it is easy to lose sight of what is important.

To be effective, your board's approach to compensation must be based on a clearly articulated philosophy that answers the following questions: How is CEO compensation intended to further stakeholder interests and facilitate accomplishing the vision, goals, and strategies? At what level, relative to executives in similar organizations, should the CEO's base salary be set? That is, as a general rule, does your board want to pay above, at, or below the market? What proportion of total compensation should be based on performance and what criteria should be employed to determine the amount of incentive compensation? What type and amount of fringe benefits are provided? What are the terms and conditions of the CEO's severance package?

We recommend the following:

- CEO compensation should be viewed as an important investment in the organization's future, not an expense. Value added to the organization by the CEO should be a huge multiple of total compensation. Your board must be prudent, but not penny-wise and pound foolish.

- Your board must have a clear rationale for the amount of CEO compensation provided and how it is determined. Internal Revenue Service guidelines for nonprofit organizations prohibit compensation arrangements that amount to private inurement or the distribution of excess revenue that should be employed to benefit stakeholders. Compensation judged to be "unreasonable" or "unjustified" can result in civil penalties and may jeopardize the organization's tax-exempt status.

- Specific terms of the compensation arrangement should be codified in a written employment contract.

Avoiding a Common CEO Compensation Mistake

The board of a small nonprofit hospital in a rural area was discussing a proposal to increase the CEO's compensation. "If we do that," one member said, "then she will be making more than anyone in the community . . . even Bob, general manager of the major supermarket in town." "Well then," another member responded, "maybe we should get Bob to run the hospital!"

Often, boards will compare a CEO's compensation to their own salary or how much executives of other businesses in the area are paid. It is important for members to understand that this is an inappropriate standard. What you should be looking at is the compensation of executives in organizations similar to yours in the market or region where your board would have to compete for talent if the present CEO left.

Principle 20

Should the need arise, the board is willing to terminate the CEO's employment.

A CEO's employment relationship can be severed for four reasons: death or disability, retirement, voluntary departure to take another position, or forced termination. While your board accepts the first three (typically with regret), it must initiate the last.

Your board must have confidence in and support the CEO. When this is no longer possible, and the situation is deemed to be irreversible, the CEO must be removed without undue delay. Stringing out the process deflects the attention of your board, causes unnecessary conflict, impairs the functioning of other managers and staff, slows down the organization, and is unfair to the CEO.

Termination should be for "cause," of which there are three:

- Disregard for your board's responsibility and authority, demonstrated by the CEO's repeatedly and consciously violating board policies and directives

- Inability to meet your board's performance expectations and facilitate fulfilling the vision, accomplishing goals, pursuing core strategies, and meeting financial objectives

- Illegal or unethical behavior

With the exception of illegal or unethical behavior, a decision to terminate the CEO should never be made on the basis of a single incident or outcome.

Termination must be handled with dignity and respect, recognizing the CEO's past efforts and accomplishments.

	low	medium	high
1. My board understands the nature and importance of its responsibility for ensuring high levels of executive performance.	1	2	3

	no		yes
2. The CEO is the only employee who is directly accountable to my board.	1		3

	low	medium	high
3. My board would be able to undertake an effective CEO recruitment and selection process if the need arose.	1	2	3

(continued)

4. My board has a comprehensive CEO   no   medium   yes
    succession plan.   1   2   3

5. My board has specified its key   low   medium   high
    performance expectations of the CEO.   1   2   3

6. Employing specific criteria, my board low   medium   high
    annually assesses the CEO's performance 1   2   3
    and provides explicit feedback and
    coaching.

7. My board employs a formal process to   low   medium   high
    annually adjust the CEO's compensation. 1   2   3

8. Should the need arise, my board would low   medium   high
    be prepared to terminate the CEO's   1   2   3
    employment relationship.

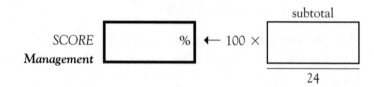

subtotal

SCORE   [%] ← 100 × [   ]
Management

24

Check-Up 3.2. Executive Performance.

Scoring: Respond to these items only if your organization has a CEO. Total your responses, divide by 24, and then multiply by 100. The product is your board's percentage of maximum performance in this area.

Getting Started: Executive Performance

• Consider meeting in executive session without the CEO present several times a year. Schedule this so it is a planned periodic event, and recognized as such by the CEO. This is your board's opportunity to talk candidly about the CEO's performance (both positives and negatives) and what should be done to continually enhance it. The chair should then provide the CEO with feedback and recommendations.

- If your board does not have a CEO succession plan, formulate one.

- Craft an initial set of CEO performance expectations. Identify the most important things the CEO must do and accomplish in order to be judged as successful by your board.

- Consider getting some outside help to work with your board design and implement an effective CEO compensation system. There is an added benefit here: the CEO can leverage the consultant's work to design or redesign the assessment and compensation of other managers and key staff.

- If your board does not have an employment contract with the CEO, develop one.
- Arrange a time in a relaxed setting where your board has a candid conversation with the CEO about the strengths and weaknesses of the board-CEO relationship and what should be done to enhance it.

QUALITY
Principle 21

The board understands that it is ultimately responsible for ensuring the quality of the organization's services or products.

Before your board can discharge its responsibility for quality, members must understand why they must assume it. There are four reasons:

First, a board's responsibility to ensure quality stems from the contract that exists between all organizations, especially nonprofits, and society. Organizations are chartered by society; additionally, nonprofits are often provided special privileges such as certain types of tax exemption. Accordingly, they are expected to provide quality services and products that meet society's needs. Boards are responsible for seeing this is the case.

Quality: Bringing It Home

Of the reasons why your board must attend to quality, none is more compelling or basic than the moral and ethical imperative. Why is your board ultimately responsible and accountable for quality? Consider this question in light of why you chose to serve on the board. Chances are you felt the organization was important, that it provided needed (if not critical) services, and you wanted to make a contribution to ensuring they were high quality. The fundamental reason most board members decide to serve and continue serving is to make certain the organization does what it's supposed to do, as well as it can.

Second, organizations are legally liable for the quality of their products and services. They can be sued when products and services are unsafe and endanger clients. Boards, being ultimately responsible for all of an organization's affairs, are expected to ensure quality and will be held accountable if it is unacceptable.

Third, for some organizations, legislative, regulatory, and accrediting bodies in addition to the courts prescribe that boards bear responsibility for quality. This is true for hospitals nationwide and (although varying from state to state) is often the case for nonprofits that provide certain social services. As a consequence, your board should be familiar with legal and regulatory mandates applicable to its type of organization.

Fourth, a board's responsibility for quality flows from its responsibility for the organization's financial health (to be addressed in principles 25–29). Poor financial performance typically results when a school or university offers poor quality education, a hospital offers inadequate medical care, a symphony orchestra schedules concerts no one wants to hear, a church provides services that are not spiritually uplifting and empowering. Conversely, an organization that provides needed services that are valued by clients and high in quality will (everything else equal) be financially viable.

To thrive and grow, let alone survive, organizations must delight their clients by providing needed and high-quality offerings. To fulfill its responsibility, your board must

- Have a shared working definition of quality, specific to the organization

- Formulate quality objectives and associated indicators

- Ensure the organization has a plan for continually improving quality

Principle 22

The board has an explicit and precise working definition of quality.

Before your board can ensure quality, it must define it.

Quality is an elusive concept because it often means different things to different people. However, if your board is unable to define quality, it will be unable to measure it; and things that are not measured cannot be consistently and continuously improved.

Thus the challenge is to develop an explicit and precise working definition of quality that provides the foundation for measuring, continuously improving, and (ultimately) ensuring it.

One of the best ways to begin conceptualizing and defining quality is to consider it from different perspectives. Here are a few illustrations in the context of a college or university:

- *Students* . . . curriculum value in terms of obtaining a good job or getting into graduate school, social life, and extracurricular activities

- *Parents* . . . safety of the environment, proper socialization

- *Faculty* . . . student competency and motivation, academic freedom, ability to pursue research interests, salary levels

- *Administration* . . . academic ranking, research and philanthropic funding, competitiveness (in attracting desirable students)

- *Alumni* . . . winning sports teams, breadth of cultural events provided

Your organization's key stakeholders and clients will have differing notions of quality. These divergent perspectives should be viewed as an opportunity rather than a problem. They provide the means for your board to develop a working definition of quality.

The process is one of *triangulation*—literally, getting a navigational fix by measurements taken from different directions simultaneously. It entails identifying key stakeholder and client groups, and then understanding what each group wants and expects. Based on this, it further requires developing a listing of quality specifications, prioritizing these specifications, and shaping them into your board's working definition of quality—and then periodically redefining quality as needs and expectations change.

Employing this process, quality is defined practically and specifically; for a particular organization on the basis of what's important to its stakeholders and clients. The resulting definition grounds and focuses your board in fulfilling its responsibility for quality.

Principle 23

The board develops a panel of quality indicators.

Defining quality is the foundation for measuring and monitoring, which in turn provide the basis for assessment. Measuring and monitoring are the focus here; how your board should assess quality in addition to ends, management and financial health will be addressed in the section of Chapter Four dealing with your board's oversight role (principle 34).

To measure the quality of something, it must be decomposed; specific aspects and associated indicators of quality have to be specified. Here is where an explicit, precise definition based on the perspective of various stakeholders and clients is critical. For example, the quality of a restaurant meal is composed of being seated promptly, attentiveness of the waiter, presentation, tastiness of the food, and atmospherics and ambience. Each of these aspects can be converted into a measurable quality indicator.

Progressing from a definition of quality to developing quality indicators is important for several reasons. First, it imposes discipline and rigor, increasing the specificity of what your board really means by quality. Second, it makes the concept of quality more concrete, meaningful, and understandable. Third, it provides a mutually agreed-to format for measuring and monitoring quality. Fourth, it is the basis for performing the quality aspect of your board's oversight role.

To develop indicators, your board must revisit its definition of quality. Each dimension and aspect must be converted into one or more quantifiable elements. The boxed text provides an illustration.

Illustrative Quality Indicators (for a College or University)

DIMENSION OR ASPECT	INDICATOR
Academic ranking	• Annual ratings published by the National Association of Colleges and Universities (for example, class I, II, III, or IV universities)
Student demand	• Ratio of applications to admissions
Entering student ability	• Average SAT scores for the freshman class
Diversity	• Proportion of the student body designated as ethnic minorities

Course quality	• Average student ratings on evaluation forms for all courses taught by level
Faculty research productivity	• Average annual grant funding per full-time tenured faculty member
Athletic team performance	• Annual win-loss percentage in specified intercollegiate sports
Philanthropy	• Annual value of gifts
	• Total value of the endowment fund

We recommend developing between one and two dozen quality indicators that are monitored by your board at least quarterly. The list should be reviewed periodically and modified if necessary. By far the best way to portray such indicators is graphically across time. Additionally, the specific indicators always mean more when juxtaposed against a standard, which might be the organization's own past performance, averages for peer group institutions, or some type of benchmark.

Principle 24

The board ensures the organization has a plan for improving quality.

Your board is ultimately responsible not only for the quality of products and services per se but also for the effective functioning of the organization's quality improvement effort. To succeed, the organization must have strategic, operational, and financial plans. These plans are developed by management and periodically reviewed by your board. This must be the case with quality. Accordingly, we recommend that management annually submit to your board its plan for managing and continuously improving quality in addition to a description of systems that are in place for doing so.

1. My board understands the importance and nature of its responsibility for ensuring quality of the organization's products and services.

   low   medium high
    1   2   3

2. My board has formulated a precise and explicit working definition of quality.

   low   medium high
    1   2   3

3. My board has specified a set of measurable quality indicators.

   low   medium high
    1   2   3

4. My board annually reviews the organization's plans for managing and continuously improving quality.

   low   medium high
    1   2   3

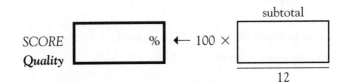

$$\text{SCORE }\textit{Quality}\quad \boxed{\%}\ \leftarrow 100 \times \frac{\boxed{}\ \text{subtotal}}{12}$$

Check-Up 3.3. Quality.

Scoring: Respond to all items. Total your responses, divide by 12, and then multiply by 100. The product is your board's percentage of maximum performance in this area.

Getting Started: Quality

- Conduct a discussion regarding why your board should be ultimately responsible and accountable for quality. How much has your board been concerned with quality in the past? How is attending to quality linked with your board's obligation to stakeholders and with its responsibility for formulating organizational ends and ensuring financial health? What is the quality of the organization's products and services? Have they been increasing or decreasing over time? How do you know? On what basis does your board make judgments about quality?

- Taking into consideration the perspectives of various key stakeholders and client groups, develop a rough working definition of quality for the organization. Formulate this definition as a list of product or service attributes.

- Specify an initial set of key indicators that your board should employ to measure and monitor quality.

- Ask management to talk with your board about its plans for improving quality and the systems that are in place to execute them.

FINANCES
Principle 25

The board understands it is ultimately responsible for the organization's financial health.

Money is simultaneously the organization's source of buoyancy and propellant. Your board must make sure there is enough money and that it is allocated in effective and legitimate ways. Your board is accountable to stakeholders for advancing and protecting the organization's financial health.

To fulfill this responsibility your board must specify key financial objectives, ensure that management-developed budgets will accomplish financial objectives, and develop financial performance indicators. Your board also needs to ensure that necessary financial controls are in place and functioning effectively.

Principle 26

The board specifies key financial objectives for the organization.

Responsibility for the money begins with answering three questions: What is your board's definition of financial health? What must the organization accomplish financially to fulfill its vision and accomplish key goals? How should financial performance be assessed?

Each year your board, assisted by its finance committee (see principle 44), with input and counsel from the CEO, should formulate a set of financial objectives for the organization. They should be comprehensive, covering all areas of financial performance and health; precise and explicit, stating what your board expects; specifically linked to the vision and key goals; and quantifiable, so it is possible to measure the extent to which they have been accomplished.

Financial objectives should be developed in four areas:

- *Bottom line:* quarterly and year-end operating and nonoperating margins for the organization as a whole (and if appropriate, major lines of business or organizational components)

- *Cash:* the amount of cash that should be available by quarter and at year-end

- *Capital:* the relative priority that should be given to major investments in facilities and equipment

- *Performance:* targets for an array of ratios (calculated from the balance sheet and income/expense statement) that measure specific aspects of financial results

Illustrations of financial objectives are provided in the boxed text.

Illustrative Financial Objectives

- The organization is expected to achieve an overall net profit from operations of at least X.X percent of gross revenue.
- Operating revenues will grow at the rate of not less than X percent per year.
- The organization will achieve a return on equity of not less than XX percent.

- The net yield on investment income (adjusted for inflation, less commissions and advisory fees) will be at least X.X percent per year.

Clear and precise financial objectives convey what your board expects, and provide management with the framework and guidelines they need to develop financial plans.

Principle 27

The board ensures that management-devised budgets are aligned with financial objectives, key goals, and the vision.

Budgets are plans for allocating organizational resources to achieve financial objectives. They come in several varieties, as the box illustrates. As with the formulation of strategy (principle 12), your board should not become directly involved in developing budgets; this is a task best performed by management.

Types of Budgets

An *operating budget* forecasts the revenue generated and the expenses incurred by the organization. It consolidates detailed financial plans prepared for the organization as a whole and for individual lines of business, departments, and programs.

A *cash budget* forecasts the sources and uses of cash. It projects quarterly cash receipts, disbursements, and beginning and ending balances.

A *capital budget* details planned expenditures for additions, modifications, and renovations to plant and for the purchase or lease of new equipment.

Management's financial planning culminates in the preparati of annual operating, cash, and capital budgets, which boards a typically required to review and approve. Overwhelmed by such budgets' weight, detail, and complexity—and the amount of effort that went into preparing them—boards often address this task as more symbolic than substantive. But how then does your board exercise appropriate influence on behalf of stakeholders in this process? Here are some suggestions:

- The types of financial information and budgets management needs to run the organization are very different than those your board requires to govern it. The CEO should be requested to prepare governance friendly and focused budgets for your board's review. They should be composed of highly aggregated categories that reflect board-formulated financial objectives.

- Management should prepare a written rationale describing how the proposed allocation of resources will lead to achieving board-specified financial objectives, key goals, and the vision.

- The governance-focused budgets and accompanying rationales should be carefully analyzed by the board's finance committee (and, if necessary, sent back to management to be reworked) before being forwarded to your board for review and approval.

This process effectively subdivides management and governance responsibilities: your board formulates financial objectives, management prepares financial plans designed to achieve them, and then your board assesses the extent to which objectives and budgets are aligned.

Principle 28

The board develops a panel of financial indicators.

Board-specified financial objectives and management budgets provide the basis for measuring and monitoring the organization's financial performance. For your board to do so it must develop a set of specific quantitative indicators (through roughly the same process it did for quality, principle 23).

Financial indicators come in three varieties. One group is specifically keyed to board-formulated *financial objectives*. For example, your board specifies an objective for net margin from operations, which then becomes the indicator. If something is important enough to be stated as an objective, it warrants being converted into an indicator and measured. A second type, called *variances*, compares operating statistics and budget projections in specific categories with actual results over some period of time, typically by month or quarter. Some examples are projected versus actual volume (number of clients served or occasions of service); costs or expenses (organization-wide or by program, department, or activity); realized revenue (overall or by service or product category); overtime hours; number of full-time equivalent personnel on the payroll. The third group, *ratios*, is statistics calculated from the organization's financial statements (balance sheet, income statement, cash flow statement). Standard types include: liquidity ratios, which measure ability to meet short-term obligations; activity ratios, which measure the ability of different types of assets to generate revenue; capital structure ratios, which measure ability to meet long-term obligations; and profitability ratios, which measure ability to generate margins from operations.

A set of financial objective, variance, and ratio indicators should be specified by your board. They provide the means for performing the financial oversight role (addressed in Chapter Four, principle 34).

Principle 29

The board ensures that necessary financial controls are in place.

Your board is accountable for making sure that accounting systems for supplying accurate and timely financial information are in place and functioning effectively; that transactions are properly authorized, executed, and recorded; and that financial statements accurately reflect the organization's current financial status. This is accomplished through an annual audit performed by a certified public accounting firm that examines the organization's financial statements; ascertains whether procedures and practices are in accordance with generally accepted accounting principles; assesses the adequacy of financial, accounting, and control systems; and presents recommendations regarding modifications and improvements to your board and management.

To safeguard the organization's resources and ensure they are used for legitimate purposes in legitimate ways, your board must appoint the external auditor and approve the audit's scope and approach. (The accounting firm performing the audit is retained by—and is accountable to—your board, not management.) The board must also review the auditor's opinion, which presents recommendations for altering systems, procedures, and practices, and require management to devise and execute plans to correct any deficiencies.

	low	medium	high
1. My board understands the importance and nature of its responsibility for ensuring the organization's financial health.	1	2	3
2. My board has formulated key organizational financial objectives.	1	2	3

(continued)

3. My board ensures that budgets are aligned with key financial objectives.

	low	medium	high
	1	2	3

4. My board has specified a set of financial indicators.

	low	medium	high
	1	2	3

5. My board ensures that necessary financial controls are in place.

	low	medium	high
	1	2	3

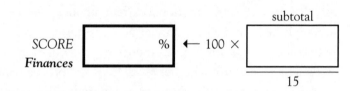

SCORE
Finances
[ ] % ← 100 × | subtotal [ ] |
15

Check-Up 3.4. Finances.

Scoring: Respond to all items. Total your responses, divide by 15, and then multiply by 100. The product is your board's percentage of maximum performance in this area.

Getting Started: Finances

- Your board must ensure that all members are able to read, understand, and interpret the organization's basic financial statements. This can be accomplished by an in-service education program (led by the organization's chief financial officer or an individual from the public accounting firm that conducts the audit). Additionally, there are a number of self-help books designed for those who want a very basic and practical introduction to finance and accounting. The single greatest impediment to a board's exercising its responsibility for finances is when members do not possess foundational financial literacy. We've found that people often mask their deficiencies in this area and avoid seeking help.

- The place for your board to begin assuming greater responsibility for finances is formulating financial objectives. Devote a portion of an upcoming meeting discussing your board's definition of financial health; then specify the most important half-dozen financial objectives that must be accomplished for the organization to be healthy.

- Develop an initial set of indicators for key financial objectives, variances, and ratios. Begin with a basic list and add to it over time.

- As a standard practice, we think it is a good idea for the board chair to review and approve all organizational disbursements to the CEO (for travel, entertainment, and the like). This reinforces accountability and takes the pressure off other employees who might find it difficult to question the CEO's expense reports.

- After the auditors have presented their opinion and report (typically at a board meeting), make sure that your board has an opportunity to meet with them in executive session, absent the CEO and other management staff. This gives your board the chance to have a candid conversation with the auditor about the organization's financial practices.

SELF
Principle 30

The board is ultimately responsible for itself—for its own performance and contributions.

To fulfill its responsibilities, your board must have effective and efficient structure, composition, and infrastructure. Principles regarding these aspects of governance will be addressed in Chapters Five, Six, and Seven.

OTHER FUNCTIONS BOARDS CAN PERFORM

This chapter has focused on a core set of responsibilities that boards must fulfill to meet their obligations. These responsibilities are functionally necessary and mandated by statutory and case law.

There are many other tasks that boards can (and, depending on the circumstances, should) choose to do that are not typically considered core governance responsibilities. Among them are

- Making personal contributions to the organization

- Participating in fundraising activities

- Serving as organizational advocates

- Providing advice and counsel to the CEO regarding the execution of the managerial role

- Performing operational tasks

These are not core governing functions per se, because they are not necessary for meeting fiduciary obligations. Yet they add value and are areas where boards can make significant contributions.

Here are a few thoughts about such tasks your board might want to consider. Board members have the right, and may be encouraged, to make personal contributions to the organization. However, such contributions should never be a prerequisite for being nominated to or continuing to serve on the board.

Board members often have access to potential donors. Because of their commitment to, investment in, and knowledge of the organization, members can be valuable in soliciting contributions. However, fundraising should be viewed as a supplemental activity of the board; it should never overwhelm, displace, or jeopardize fulfilling its core responsibilities. Fundraising is a distinctive organizational function that is often most effectively conducted by a separate organization or subsidiary (a foundation) with its own board.

Serving as an advocate for the organization is something that should be expected of all board members. However, members should be very careful about speaking on behalf of the organization; too many people doing so in an uncoordinated way can send confusing and conflicting messages that do far more harm than good. When advocacy to key external constituents on important issues is necessary, consider having the board chair, accompanied by the CEO, make the presentation.

CEOs often, and appropriately, seek counsel from the board chair and individual members on substantive issues related to the performance of their managerial role. Because of their familiarity with the organization (in addition to standing outside it), members can often be very helpful. But the key here is that when providing such counsel members are not acting in a governance capacity, and their advice can be either taken or rejected.

Particularly in small nonprofit organizations, board members are often called upon to do double duty: governing in addition to performing tasks typically done by staff and employees. When a nonprofit organization lacks resources and calls upon board members to do such work, we recommend that an explicit and precise distinction be made that they are doing so as individual volunteers, completely separate from their role as board members.

The overarching principle that flows through all of the preceding recommendations is this: the defining and fundamental function of a board and board members is governing the organization and fulfilling core responsibilities (for ends, management, quality, finances and the board itself) necessary to do so. Board members may be called upon to perform other tasks and may choose to do so. But when they engage in such tasks, they are functioning outside of and separate from their positions as board members.

4

Functioning
Roles

This chapter focuses on the second half of governance functioning, roles—activities your board must perform to fulfill its
responsibilities.

Principle 31

**The board understands that to govern effectively it must
execute three core roles: policy formulation, decision making,
and oversight.**

If you walk into a meeting of a high-performance board (one that
employs the principles presented in Chapter Three) and ask what
it is doing, the response should be: "We are fulfilling our responsibilities for ends, executive performance, quality, finances, and our
own functioning." But *how* does the board actually do this? The answer: by performing three core roles:

- *Policy formulation:* specifying expectations, directives,
  and constraints

- *Decision making:* choosing among alternatives regarding
  matters that require board attention, input, or approval

- *Oversight:* monitoring and assessing organizational
  processes and outcomes

Thus governance work involves formulating policy, making decisions, and overseeing ends, executive performance, quality, finances, and the board's own performance and contributions. It's a two-sided coin. Fulfilling responsibilities is the what, or substantive, aspect of governance; executing roles is the how, or activity, aspect.

Principle 32

The board formulates policies regarding its ultimate responsibilities.

Policy Governance

Our ideas about a board's policy formulation role have been influenced by the work of John Carver. If you want a more in-depth treatment of policy as governance tool, we recommend his books — *Boards That Make a Difference: A New Design for Leadership in Nonprofit and Public Organizations; Reinventing Your Board: A Step-by-Step Guide to Implementing Policy Governance;* and *CarverGuide 1: Basic Principles of Policy Governance.* All are published by Jossey-Bass; to order call 800-956-7739. "Policy Governance®" is a registered service mark of John Carver.

Policy formulation is the best tool your board has to influence the organization and to make sure that it benefits — and advances the interests of — its stakeholders. Additionally, explicitly formulated policies provide tangible evidence that your board is fulfilling its responsibilities.

Board policies are declarative statements that direct, guide, and constrain subsequent decisions and actions. They are mechanisms for performing two absolutely essential governance functions. First, expressing your board's expectations of the organization, management, and itself—thus conveying what your board wants done (acceptable methods) and accomplished (desired results). Second, specifying authority and tasks delegated by your board to management. Illustrative board policies are presented in Resource B.

The most important matters about which your board must formulate policy are its responsibilities.

Your board fulfills its *responsibilities for ends* by formulating policies about these key areas:

- *Stakeholders:* who they are

- *Vision:* the organization's core purposes and values; what it should become, at its very best, in the future

- *Goals:* key things that must be accomplished to fulfill the vision

- *Alignment:* how management strategies should be linked to goals and the vision

Your board fulfills its responsibility for *ensuring high levels of executive performance* by formulating policies about these issues:

- *Succession:* what should be done when the CEO position becomes vacant

- *Standards:* performance expectations of the CEO

- *Assessment:* procedures and indicators used to evaluate CEO performance

- *Compensation:* the method employed to adjust the CEO's salary, incentive pay, and benefits

Your board fulfills its *responsibility for ensuring quality* by formulating policies about these aspects of quality:

- *Definition:* what constitutes quality

- *Standards:* criteria employed to assess product or service quality and client satisfaction

- *Methods:* systems that must be in place to monitor and improve quality

Your board fulfills its *responsibility for ensuring the organization's financial health* by formulating policies about funds and their use:

- *Financial objectives:* what must be achieved financially to accomplish key organizational goals and fulfill the vision

- *Budgets:* the nature of management's task of devising financial plans and their alignment with board-specified financial objectives, key goals, and the vision

- *Controls:* procedures that must be in place to ensure organizational resources are legitimately deployed and accounted for

Your board *assumes responsibility for its own effectiveness and efficiency* (topics addressed in Chapters Five through Seven) by formulating these internal policies:

- *Structure:* how governance work is subdivided and coordinated

- *Composition:* needed board member characteristics, competencies, capacities, and expectations

- *Infrastructure:* resources and systems required to support the board and its work

As illustrated in Figure 4.1, there are four types of policies. Your board can convey its expectations and directives by being prescriptive (stating its "thou shalts") or by being prohibitive (stating its

	Results	Methods
Prescriptions	Policies that prescribe certain results	Policies that prescribe certain methods
Prohibitions	Policies that prohibit certain results	Policies that prohibit certain methods

Figure 4.1. Types of Board Policy.

"thou shalt nots"). Additionally, policies can focus on either results or methods.

Your board can either prohibit or prescribe both results and methods. However, we have found the most effective policies *prescribe results* and *prohibit methods*. Results are what your board wants accomplished. The best way of conveying such expectations is simply stating them; saying, "achieve this." As a general rule, your board should avoid specifying methods. There are an infinite number of them; getting involved in determining the way results should be achieved bogs your board down in detail, and prescribing one method eliminates all others. Additionally, doing so brings your board dangerously near, if not across, the line that separates governing from managing. Therefore, if your board has the need to express its expectations regarding methods, we recommend formulating policies that restrict, limit, and prohibit, denoting those that are unacceptable.

Your board's policies should be formulated with great care. Board policy statements are an organization's most important pronouncements, so they should be carefully crafted. They should also be

Responsibility area: Policy number: _____10.2_____

[ ] ends
                                        Page __1__ of __1__
[ ] executive performance
                                        Date of origination __10-25-02__
[ ] quality

[✓] finances   Review: _____every year_____

[ ] self (governance structure,
    composition and infrastructure)

Issue: criteria to be employed for selecting/reappointing the audit firm

Policy statement:

_____
_____
_____
_____
_____
_____
_____
_____
_____
_____
_____
_____

Figure 4.2. Board Policy Form.

expressed powerfully. Equivocal language (words such as *may*, *might*, *should*, or *could*) must be avoided. Forcefulness is necessary for your board's directives to be attended to and heeded. And they must be written for all to see. Absent this, your board's policies are nothing more than hot air. Additionally, they should be presented in a common format; Figure 4.2 provides an example that your board might want to employ.

In addition to being carefully crafted, authoritative, and codified in a consistent form, board policy statements need to be brief. Wordiness confuses rather than clarifies. To be understood and have the desired impact, policies must be easily digestible — typically expressed in less than one page.

The set of policies must be both minimalist and comprehensive. That is, when it comes to policy less is better than more. Your board should formulate as few policies as possible to convey what it expects regarding each of its responsibilities. The noise caused by too many policies obscures what is really important. Despite the need for parsimony, however, your board must weigh in regarding its most important expectations and directives across the full range of responsibilities, leaving no big gaps. For example, it's ineffective to formulate policies regarding financial objectives without policies regarding key goals and the vision.

Outmoded and outdated board policies must be tossed out or modified. Nothing depreciates the quality and power of your board's voice quite so much as policies that have been rendered irrelevant by changed circumstances or the passage of time. We recommend conducting an audit of all board policies every several years, eliminating those that are no longer needed or relevant.

Principle 33

The board makes decisions regarding matters requiring its attention and input.

Decisions, Decisions . . . Some Illustrations

- Are management strategies aligned with key goals and the vision? Should they be approved? [decision making regarding *ends*]

- Should a representative from a key stakeholder be offered a board seat? [decision making regarding governance *obligations* and *ends*]

- To what extent did the CEO meet board-specified performance objectives last year? How much of a bonus should be awarded? [decision making regarding *executive performance*]

- Since they have been achieved or surpassed for the last three years, should client satisfaction standards be increased? [decision making regarding *quality*]

- Should a new audit firm be retained? [decision making regarding *finances*]

- Should the board develop a methodology to assess the performance and contribution of its members? [decision making regarding *self*]

Ask boards about the most important things they do, and the answer is typically, "Make decisions." Decisions like those illustrated in the boxed text, are important; your board must make them. However, they should be grounded on, flow from, and be shaped by policy. Your board must first formulate policies regarding key issues for each of its responsibilities, and then determine what needs to be decided. Absent this approach, decisions are often idiosyncratic, disjointed, conflicting, and ineffective.

Boards have four decision-making options, all of which may be in use simultaneously:

- *Option #1*: Retaining authority and making decisions itself.

- *Option #2*: Requesting proposals and recommendations from management before making a decision.

- *Option #3*: Delegating decision-making authority with constraints; decisions are handed off to management, but with imposed limitations. For example, your board allows the CEO to move funds from one capital budget category to another as long as they are less than a specified dollar amount; if the transfer exceeds this limit, the CEO must seek board approval.

• *Option #4:* Delegating decision making by exception. Management is authorized to make all decisions in a given area, with the exception of those that have been either expressly prohibited or reserved by the board.

Here are some suggestions for enhancing your board's decision-making effectiveness:

Make as few decisions as possible. This somewhat counterintuitive recommendation is consistent with the notion that your board, in executing its roles, should focus on policy formulation rather than decision making. As you pay more attention to policy issues and formulate better policies, the number of decisions that have to be made at the board level decreases dramatically.

Do not fall into the trap of ratifying decisions that have been appropriately made by management. There are two problems here. First, this practice wastes a lot of time. Second, when a management decision is ratified by your board, it becomes your board's decision and accountability is shifted.

Make only organization-defining and vision-critical decisions, unless others are mandated by law or regulation. Due to severe limitations on its time and attention, your board must focus on decisions that matter most and those where it can really add value. This demands tremendous discipline as it is easy to become drawn into arenas that are important but do not require board-level involvement.

Decision proposals forwarded by management should be reviewed by a board committee before being placed on the agenda for action. Recommendations arrive at the boardroom door as complex weighty documents with important implications for the organization. (If they do not, they should not be placed before the board!) In even the very best boards, many members may not have the knowledge, expertise, and experience—or for that matter, the patience—to evaluate these proposals thoroughly. Consequently, committees must provide decision-making preparation by investigating, seeking justification, questioning assumptions, and exploring options

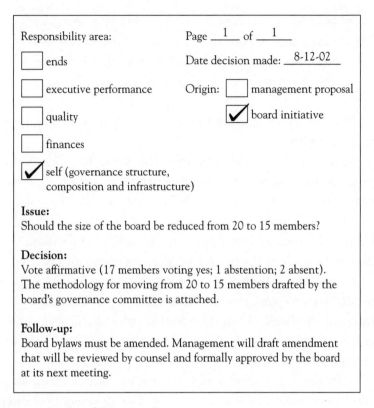

Responsibility area:	Page __1__ of __1__
☐ ends	Date decision made: __8-12-02__
☐ executive performance	Origin: ☐ management proposal
☐ quality	☑ board initiative
☐ finances	
☑ self (governance structure, composition and infrastructure)	

Issue:
Should the size of the board be reduced from 20 to 15 members?

Decision:
Vote affirmative (17 members voting yes; 1 abstention; 2 absent). The methodology for moving from 20 to 15 members drafted by the board's governance committee is attached.

Follow-up:
Board bylaws must be amended. Management will draft amendment that will be reviewed by counsel and formally approved by the board at its next meeting.

Figure 4.3. Board Decision Form.

prior to the issue's being discussed, deliberated, and acted upon by your board.

Codify all decisions. If they are important enough to be made, they should be documented. Board decisions often slip away—either not captured or embedded in the minutes. The board's voice must be recorded in order to convey its directives. Figure 4.3 shows a form for capturing your board's decisions.

These forms should be consolidated in a ring binder (with tabs for each governance responsibility) and periodically distributed to all board members.

Each year, conduct an audit of your board's decisions. Some questions that should be asked: Are decisions policy-based and consistent? Are they the type of decisions your board should be making (in terms of their importance and your board's ability to add value)? Did your board have to make them or could they have been better and more appropriately made by management? If a decision dealt with a proposal forwarded by management, was it thoroughly analyzed by a committee prior to full board deliberation and action? Are there decisions that could have been avoided if a board policy had been in place? Have any decisions created de facto policies that should have been deliberated and acted upon as such?

Principle 34

The board oversees (monitors and assesses) key organizational processes and outcomes.

The dashboard of your car does not provide a lot of information, but try driving with no gas gauge, speedometer, odometer, battery indicator, oil pressure light, or engine thermometer. Feedback is essential for altering what your board does and how well it's done. However, most boards attempt to govern without well-designed dashboards containing the right type of gauges. Driving partially blind, they lack information needed to ascertain whether things are working out as planned, promised, and expected.

In executing its oversight role, your board monitors and assesses key organizational process and outcomes. This provides the means to answer four questions: Is the organization performing in a manner that advances stakeholder interests? Are your board's expectations and directives, as specified in its policies, being met? Are your board's decisions having the desired impact? Are your board's constraints being respected as management performs delegated tasks?

As illustrated in Figure 4.4 and the boxed text, the board oversight process has five steps:

1. *Select indicators.* There are a multitude of things your board could choose to monitor and assess. What should attention

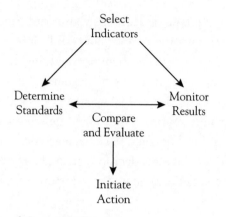

Figure 4.4. Board Oversight Process.

be focused upon? What must your board oversee to ensure accountability and obtain the feedback it needs to govern?

2. *Specify standards.* For each indicator, what does your board
   expect? What constitutes exemplary, adequate, or unacceptable levels of performance?

3. *Monitor results.* For each indicator, gather data that answers
   the question: What actually happened?

4. *Compare and evaluate the results against the standards.* For each
   indicator, how did what actually happened measure up to
   what the board wanted?

5. *Take action.* What should be done if there is a difference between the standard and the result for a particular indicator?

Illustration: Board Oversight

INDICATOR: Present value of new donations

- *Standard:*   3 percent of yearly net operating revenue.

- *Result:*   1.5 percent.

- *Comparison:*   Target not met.

- *Action:*   Request analysis and plan from management to
                     be presented at board meeting on [date].

INDICATOR: Non-exempt employee turnover

- *Standard:*   Less than 15 percent of adjusted full-time equiva-
                     lent employees per year.

- *Result:*   12.5 percent for the most recent year.

- *Comparison:*   Standard exceeded.

- *Action:*   Reward and celebrate.

INDICATOR: Net operating margin

- *Standard:*   5 percent.

- *Result:*   2.5 percent for the last six months of the current
                     fiscal year.

- *Comparison:*   Performance 50 percent under target; standard
                     not met.

- *Action:*   Management analysis and plan to enhance rev-
                     enues or reduce costs to be presented at the next
                     board finance committee; net operating margin re-
                     port and analysis to be forwarded to the board
                     quarterly (rather than semiannually as has been
                     the past practice).

INDICATOR: Average regularly scheduled board meeting ab-
                     sentee rate

- *Standard:*   Not to exceed 15 percent (both excused and un-
                     excused absences).

- *Result:*   22 percent over last four meetings.

- *Comparison:*   Standard not met.

- *Action:*   Attendance record to be distributed to all board
                     members quarterly; chair to meet with members
                     who have missed more than four meetings in the
                     last year to discuss their level of participation.

Your board must take the initiative in specifying the type of information it requires to effectively execute its oversight role. Although management must be involved (providing perspective, expertise, and support), this responsibility rests squarely with your board; only it can determine which indicators and standards are needed to oversee in a manner that ensures accountability.

What dashboards does your board need? At minimum, we recommend five sets of indicators and associated standards, one for each board responsibility: ends, executive performance, quality, finances, and self. We have worked with many boards in designing dashboard systems. Here are a few of the important things we've learned:

- If something is important enough for your board to express as a policy, it warrants monitoring and assessment.

- If your board attempts to monitor and assess too many things, it will oversee nothing particularly well. We recommend developing about a dozen indicators for each board responsibility.

- A standard must be attached to each indicator, specifying levels of unacceptable, adequate, and exemplary performance. That is, your board's most important expectations (conveyed in its policies) drive the selection of both indicators and standards. For example, consider a typical board policy regarding overall financial performance: "The net margin from operations must exceed 10 percent." The indicator is net margin from operations, the standard is 10 percent.

- Indicators must be quantifiable. If something is not measurable it cannot be monitored. However, it's important to keep in mind that most subjective performance indicators can be quantified. For example, employee satisfaction (inherently subjective) can be

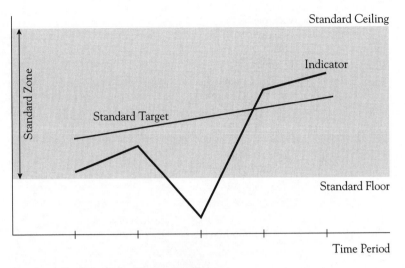

Figure 4.5. Oversight Reporting Format.

measured by an appropriately designed, administered, and analyzed questionnaire.

- Remember that data becomes information only when it is organized. We've found the best method is graphical. Figure 4.5 illustrates a format we have found useful.

Picture your board's dashboard system as a three-ring binder with five dividers labeled Ends, Management, Quality, Finances, and Self. Behind each divider are about twelve pieces of paper, each tracking a different indicator and conveying an associated standard (in the form portrayed in Figure 4.5).

Principle 35

When it meets, the board spends the majority of its time performing its policy formulation, decision-making, and oversight roles.

How much of your board meeting time is spent passively listening? That is, sitting there while someone provides background

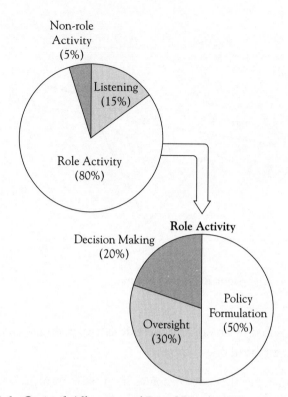

Figure 4.6. Optimal Allocation of Board Meeting Time.

information, briefings, presentations, reports (from management, staff, consultants, and the board's own committees). We estimate the figure exceeds 60 percent for most boards. Listening is important. But could your board really govern, make a difference, and add value if it spent 100 percent of its time just listening? The answer is clearly no.

One of the best indicators of a board's strength is the proportion of its meeting time spent discussing, deliberating, and debating policies, decisions, and oversight parameters regarding its responsibilities.

Figure 4.6 depicts the distribution of effort we consider optimal. Notice total meeting time is 80 percent role-related activity, 15 percent listening, and 5 percent non–role-related activity (including socializing and down time). Fifty percent of role-related activity is spent formulating policy, 30 percent engaged in oversight, and 20 percent making decisions.

Principle 36

The board acts only collectively; and once it does so, members support its policies and decisions.

We noted in Chapter One that governance is a "team sport." When your board acts, it must do so as a group. Individual members have absolutely no power; authority derives from your board as a whole. Members can argue, deliberate, debate, and disagree with one another regarding a particular issue. But once a vote is taken, members must lock arms and support your board's decision even if they voted against it. Divisiveness depreciates the quality and clarity of your board's voice. When a member finds him- or herself continually unwilling to support your board's collective will, it is time for him or her to resign.

	low	medium	high
1. My board understands that its core roles are formulating policy, making decisions, and oversight.	1	2	3
2. My board formulates policies regarding its ultimate responsibilities.	1	2	3
3. My board makes decisions regarding issues and matters requiring its attention and input.	1	2	3
4. My board oversees (monitors and assesses) key organizational processes and outcomes.	1	2	3

(continued)

	low	medium	high
5. In meetings, my board spends the majority of time performing its roles: formulating policy, making decisions, and overseeing.	1	2	3
6. My board acts only collectively; once we act, members support our board's policies and decisions.	1	2	3

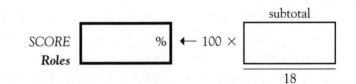

SCORE
Roles   [   ] % ← 100 × [subtotal   ]
                                  ――――――――――
                                      18

Check-Up 4.1. Roles.

Scoring: Respond to all items. Total your responses, divide by 18, and then multiply by 100. The product is your board's percentage of maximum performance in this area.

Getting Started: Roles

- If your board has not been employing policy formulation as a governance tool, begin doing so immediately. The best way to start is by framing major issues on which your board must act as proposed policies. It is the nature and substance of the policy that is discussed and voted upon at meetings. Consider employing the policy form presented in Figure 4.2.

- Most boards have policies (in one form or another), but they are embedded in meeting minutes. Scan your past minutes for the most important statements of policy, put them in the form suggested here, and have your board reconsider and act on them.

- Over the next year, make sure your board spends a portion of each meeting deliberating its key expectations in each area of responsibility (ends, management, quality, finances, and self). These discussions should then prompt the drafting of policies that reflect and codify such expectations.

- Through an examination of your minutes over the past several years, conduct an audit of your board's decisions. Codify these decisions employing the form presented in Figure 4.3. Present them to the board for review, ratification, and modification. Eliminate decisions where appropriate.

- Develop initial dashboards for each responsibility area. Focus on designing less than a half-dozen indicators and associated standards for each. The place to begin is with your board's most important expectations as conveyed in its policies.

Board Functioning, Overall

This and the previous chapter have presented principles of board functioning; the responsibilities your board must fulfill and the roles your board must perform to really govern. Taken together, they add up to an overarching principle regarding what the board needs to do to make a difference (on behalf of stakeholders) and add value (to the organization).

Principle 37

The board has an explicit, precise, coherent, and empowering notion of the type of work it must do—its responsibilities and roles.

Your board's description of its job should be codified in a charter. The boxed text provides an example.

Board Charter

Our board's obligation is to ensure the organization's resources are deployed in ways that advance and protect stakeholder interests.

To serve as the agent of stakeholders and add value to the organization, we formulate policy (convey expectations, direct, and guide), make decisions (choose among alternatives regarding matters that warrant board attention), and oversee (monitor and assess) the organization's ends, executive performance, quality, and finances, as well as the board's own performance. Our board's work is defined by these roles and responsibilities.

Our board is responsible for determining the organization's ends. To fulfill this responsibility we formulate the organization's vision; specify key goals that, if accomplished, lead to the vision being fulfilled; and ensure strategies devised by management are aligned with key goals and the vision.

Our board is responsible for ensuring high levels of executive performance. To fulfill this responsibility we select and recruit the chief executive officer (CEO); formulate CEO performance objectives; assess the CEO's performance; determine the CEO's compensation; and, should the need arise, terminate the CEO's employment. Subject to its directives and oversight, our board delegates all management functions to the CEO. The CEO is the only employee directly accountable to our board for managing the organization.

Our board is responsible for ensuring the quality of products and services provided by the organization to its clients. To fulfill this responsibility we define quality; set standards and employ them to assess quality; and ensure management has a plan for continuously improving quality.

Our board is responsible for the organization's financial health. To fulfill this responsibility we establish financial objectives; ensure financial planning is undertaken in a manner that leads to accomplishing such objectives; monitor and assess financial performance; and ensure that necessary controls are in place.

Our board is responsible for its own performance and contributions. To fulfill this responsibility we continually enhance the effectiveness and efficiency of our governance structure, composition, and infrastructure.

5

Structure

Structure is the anatomical aspect of governance — the context for your board's functioning, composition, and infrastructure. Structural issues include determining the number of boards and relationships among them, the size of the board or boards, and the number and type of board committees.

A poorly designed structure will impair your board. Similarly, an appropriate structure will facilitate (though not guarantee) effective performance of governance work.

Because an organization can have more than one board, there are two basic structural models: centralized and decentralized. In nonprofit organizations, the former is far more common than the latter.

In a centralized structure, as depicted in Figure 5.1, the organization is governed by a single board. Even if it is composed of separately incorporated subsidiary organizations, they do not have boards.

A decentralized governance structure (Figure 5.2) is defined by two characteristics: the organization has one or more separately incorporated subsidiary organizations, and these subsidiaries have their own boards. The parent board exercises ultimate authority over subsidiary boards, but governance responsibilities and roles are subdivided and shared among them. See the boxed text on page 82 for an illustration of a decentralized governance structure.

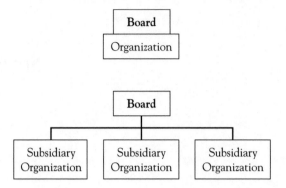

Figure 5.1. Centralized Governance Structure.

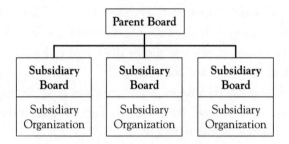

Figure 5.2. Decentralized Governance Structure.

A Decentralized Governance Structure

We recently worked with a client that had the following corporate structure:

- A national 501(c)(3) nonprofit organization.

- Seventy-three local chapters, incorporated in their respective states as 501(c)(3) nonprofit organizations.

- Some local chapters had separately incorporated 501(c)(3) foundations and for-profit subsidiaries.

The governance structure looked like this:

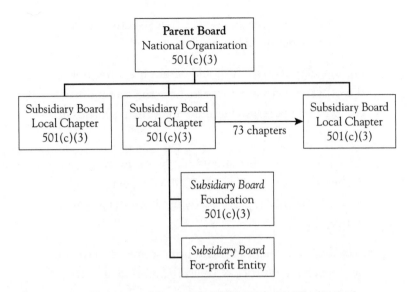

Figure 5.3. Illustrative Decentralized Governance Structure.

Most of the principles presented here apply to both centralized and decentralized governance structures. However, several are relevant only to organizations with more than one board, and are noted as such.

Principle 38

The board recognizes the importance of governance structure that is consciously designed based on explicit criteria and choices.

Structure matters. Your board must ensure that it has an appropriate structure, supporting and enabling the performance of governance work. The design of your board's structure should be guided by the following criteria:

- *Intentionality:* A great, even good, governance structure is not accidental. It is the product of careful analysis and explicit choices. Recognize that structure must be consciously designed by your board.

- *Functionality:* Function should determine form, not the other way around. Governance structure must be crafted to support and facilitate fulfilling responsibilities and performing roles.

- *Adaptability:* Structure should not be set in stone. Rather, it should be viewed as a flexible, even temporary, vehicle that is periodically modified as circumstances change.

- *Individuality:* Structure should be customized to the distinctive characteristics of your organization, and the governance challenges it faces.

Principle 39

Governance structure is streamlined.

Here, less is more. Parsimony should drive the design process, ensuring there are as few moving parts as possible.

Streamlined structure aids (but does not guarantee) that your board's limited attention, energy, and time will be focused and efficiently deployed. An overweight and cumbersome structure typically diffuses and squanders these resources. Additionally, it consumes an inordinately large amount of precious executive time. Every board and committee meeting must be prepared for, attended, staffed, documented, and followed up.

Thus, everything else being equal, the best governance structure is parsimonious, having the fewest possible boards, committees, board members, and committee members. It should be neither larger nor more complex than absolutely necessary to facilitate performance of governance work.

Principle 40

Unless there are extraordinarily compelling reasons to do otherwise, board size ranges from nine to nineteen members.

Board size is a fundamental and critical structural characteristic that significantly affects all aspects of governance functioning. Thus it should be based upon an explicit rationale and subject to periodic review.

The sizes of nonprofit boards are incredibly diverse. For example, we have worked with a five-member homeowners' association board, an eleven-person church board, a twenty-five-member board of a health system, a forty-member trade association board, and a seventy-five-member philanthropic foundation board.

Very large boards are often carryovers from times past, when their purpose was primarily—if not exclusively—fundraising. Today, other than for foundations, the central board obligation is governing, not fundraising; having a large number of members for this express purpose is unnecessary. Other common reasons given for having a large board include providing an opportunity for significant stakeholder and community involvement in governance and being able to spread an overly burdensome amount of board work (a symptom of ineffective governance) among many members.

Large boards have several strikes against them. First, they are more cumbersome deliberative and decision-making bodies than smaller ones. Second, because of this, they tend to have active and powerful executive committees, where the "real work" is done. This frequently creates a two-class system, leaving those members not on the executive committee feeling disenfranchised. Third, very large boards tend to reduce the involvement of individual members, thus decreasing their commitment. Finally, big boards tend to have more and larger committees simply to guarantee that every member has an opportunity to serve on several of them.

Very small boards have several significant disadvantages as well. First, one or two members can dominate the board and exert disproportionate influence. Second, lacking critical mass, they often fail to develop a positive group dynamic. Third, the tardiness or absence of a few members can dramatically affect the ability to get work done at board meetings. Fourth, an unexpected departure of a talented member can be disruptive due to a lack of bench strength. Fifth, they often demand too much of their members and run the risk of burning them out.

No one specific size is best for all boards, but there is an optimal range. Boards that fall outside it, being either too large or small, seriously compromise their effectiveness, efficiency, and creativity. Your board should be *large enough* to get the work done and achieve a requisite amount of diversity in terms of member characteristics, knowledge, skills, experience, and perspectives. At the same time, it should also be *small enough* to function as a cohesive, focused, and deliberative body for policy formulation, decision making, and oversight.

Our experience (supported by the results of a large body of group dynamics and performance research work) suggests the optimal board size is from nine to nineteen members. This range should be a "default setting." If your board decides to be either smaller or larger, it should have a carefully thought-out, explicit, and persuasive rationale for doing so. That is, boards smaller than nine members or larger than nineteen should be considered guilty until proven innocent. Additionally, we recommend that your board have an odd number of members to minimize the possibility of tie votes on controversial issues.

Board size in subsidiary organizations, where a decentralized governance structure is employed, is often (and quite appropriately) either above or below the optimal size range as a result of functional considerations. For example, a subsidiary organization board may have a very narrow set of tasks delegated to it by the parent. In such instances fewer members might be needed. Similarly, a subsidiary foundation (fundraising) board might be very large so as to maximize community liaison and member giving in addition to supplying a sizable workforce to solicit funds. But the overarching principle still applies: have a compelling reason for constructing boards outside the optimal range. The rationale should be explicitly tied to the board's purpose and designed to optimize its functioning. While a very small or large number of members might make sense, it is important to remember that subsidiary boards are, first and foremost, governing bodies. They have important obligations, functions, and legal duties to fulfill, and their ability to do so is impaired when their size is inappropriate.

Principle 41

If governance structure is decentralized, the authority, responsibilities, and roles of parent and subsidiary boards are explicitly and precisely specified.

Nonprofit organizations with decentralized governance structures (multiple boards with superior-subordinate relationships), face a unique challenge: governance work must be effectively and efficiently subdivided and coordinated among parent and subsidiary boards. When this is not explicitly attended to, or done poorly, significant problems can arise: policy formulation, decision making, and oversight take more time; the amount of rework increases; and conflict arises over the authority of different boards.

In organizations with decentralized governance structures, board work must be explicitly and precisely mapped (as portrayed in Figure 5.4 and illustrated in the boxed text), specifying how responsibilities and roles will be partitioned. There are three options: a specific role (policy formulation, decision making, and oversight) with respect to a given responsibility (ends, management, quality, finances, and self) can be *retained* by the parent board, *shared* by the parent and subsidiary board, or *delegated* to the subsidiary board.

	Ends	Management	Quality	Finances	Self
Policy Formulation	Parent board ↑ retain share ↓ delegate Subsidiary board	Parent board ↑ retain share ↓ delegate Subsidiary board	Parent board ↑ retain share ↓ delegate Subsidiary board	Parent board ↑ retain share ↓ delegate Subsidiary board	Parent board ↑ retain share ↓ delegate Subsidiary board
Decision Making	Parent board ↑ retain share ↓ delegate Subsidiary board	Parent board ↑ retain share ↓ delegate Subsidiary board	Parent board ↑ retain share ↓ delegate Subsidiary board	Parent board ↑ retain share ↓ delegate Subsidiary board	Parent board ↑ retain share ↓ delegate Subsidiary board
Oversight	Parent board ↑ retain share ↓ delegate Subsidiary board	Parent board ↑ retain share ↓ delegate Subsidiary board	Parent board ↑ retain share ↓ delegate Subsidiary board	Parent board ↑ retain share ↓ delegate Subsidiary board	Parent board ↑ retain share ↓ delegate Subsidiary board

Figure 5.4. Board Work Mapping in Decentralized Governance Structures.

Subdivision of Responsibilities Among Parent and Subsidiary Boards

CEO selection in subsidiary organizations: Responsibility of the parent organization CEO with input and advice provided by the subsidiary board

Specifying subsidiary organization financial objectives: Developed by the subsidiary board based on policies formulated by the parent board; subsidiary board financial objectives must contribute to accomplishing those specified by the parent board

Quality oversight in subsidiary organizations:	Indicators and standards specified by the parent board; monitoring and assessment conducted by the subsidiary board (with annual reports to the parent)
Subsidiary board composition:	Subsidiary boards recruit and nominate new board members; such members are recommended to the parent board for approval

Principle 42

If advisory bodies are employed, their functions are clearly specified and differentiated from those of governing boards.

Many nonprofit organizations have "advisory boards." This term is a misnomer as these bodies do not bear any legal fiduciary responsibility for the organization and hence do not govern. However, such bodies often behave as if they actually govern. In these situations, conflict arises between them and the governing board.

If your organization has an advisory body, its objectives and functions must be clearly defined. Here are some examples:

- Providing input to and serving as a sounding board for the board and management; such advice may be either taken or discarded

- Providing a link to the organization's stakeholders and customers

- Serving as an organizational advocate in the community

Principle 43

The board specifies the roles of committees and its relationship to them.

Few boards can function effectively and efficiently without commit-tees, as board meetings rarely provide enough time to get all the work done. Additionally, many issues can be better addressed by groups smaller than the full board. However, committees sometimes perform tasks that, legally and functionally, must be discharged by the full board. In such instances committees tend to dominate the board rather than supporting and being controlled by it.

A key issue facing your board is: How should work be subdivided and coordinated (between the board and its committees, and among these committees) in a way that facilitates effective and efficient governance, but does not compromise the board's integrity, au-thority, and responsibility?

Committees cannot be expected—and should never be al-lowed—to govern. That is, they should never fulfill responsibili-ties and perform roles that are the board's alone. This legal and fiduciary obligation rests with the full board, not its committees. With the exception of an executive committee, committees have no authority, and should never formulate policies or make deci-sions. Rather, their role is to improve the use of time, supporting and facilitating the board's functioning at meetings by performing governance staff work for the board. Committees do this by under-taking analyses and framing recommendations that serve as the ba-sis of the board's discussions, deliberation, and action.

Principle 44

The number and type of committees are designed to reflect the board's responsibilities and facilitate and support its work.

The basic questions regarding committees your board must resolve are: Which committees should we have? What should they do?

Many boards have a standing committee structure that does not change from year to year. This rigid arrangement runs the risk of freezing board focus and functioning, which can be a problem when challenges confronting the organization change. Such boards often struggle to address new issues with an increasingly outmoded committee structure.

The challenge is how to have an effective and efficient committee structure that is relevant to current conditions (which change from year to year) and reflects the board's responsibilities (which typically do not).

The solution is for your board to tailor its committee structure, and the functioning of each committee, to established priorities. This can be accomplished through a zero-based committee design process.

Zero-based design forces your board to seriously reevaluate its committees every year. It ends each year with the automatic dissolution of all committees. It then determines which, if any, previous committees should continue to exist and which new ones should be created. Only when organizational goals (principle 11) and board objectives (principle 58) have been specified can your board appropriately determine what committees, if any, it should have.

Boards employing a zero-based design typically find that some committees do continue to exist year after year, typically those that support fulfilling governance responsibilities. Although terminology varies, committees are these:

- Executive committee

- Vision and goals (or ends) committee

- Executive performance and compensation committee

- Quality committee

- Finance committee

- Governance committee

Even so, much of the value of the zero-based approach is that it forces your board to critically and explicitly assess the contribution of and need for each committee, taking none for granted. This generally produces changes in committee structure in addition to modification of individual committee charters, objectives, and work plans (addressed in principle 45).

As the committees of most boards are specified in the bylaws, any alteration in committee structure would require annual amendments of them. Since this would be excessively burdensome, we recommend a one-time bylaw revision stating your board employs a zero-based design process, configuring its committees at the beginning of each year.

Committee design should be guided by the following criteria:

- *Authority:* Only the board bears ultimate responsibility for governing the organization. Board committees, except in very limited situations (such as an executive committee that can act in defined emergency situations), have no independent authority to make decisions on behalf of the board.

- *Minimalism:* The smallest possible number of board committees should be created.

- *Functionality:* Committees are established for the purpose of assisting the board in fulfilling its responsibilities and performing its roles.

Principle 45

The functions and tasks of committees are specified by the board and codified in a charter and work plan.

Your board must do more than determine what committees it will have and specify their general authority, it must also direct them. Committees lacking focus can pull your board in many different directions at once, hindering effective governance.

Although each committee performs different functions and tasks, the sum total of these activities must converge to move your board toward the achievement of its annual objectives (see principle 58).

Your board should begin framing, directing, and constraining the work of its committees through the formulation of charters. Such charters specify committee objectives and key functions. Illustrative charters for a variety of commonly used committees are provided in Resource C.

Your board should fine-tune committee functioning by requiring that each develop an annual work plan, which is then reviewed by the executive committee and approved by your board. Work plans explicitly describe the key priorities, tasks, deliverables, and deadlines of each committee. Such plans focus a committee's efforts on important work it must perform on behalf of your board.

Principle 46

Governance structure is thoroughly assessed at regular intervals and modified if necessary.

Regular assessment is critical for ensuring governance structure is appropriate, effective, and efficient. This requires your board to look back and plan ahead, addressing questions such as these:

- What aspects of governance structures are working well? Which should be working better?

- What aspects of structure are in place just because "we have always done it that way"? Is there any reason they should not be eliminated or modified?

- What structural alterations (board size, number of boards and their relationships, number and type of committees) are needed to help us govern more effectively and efficiently?

Most evaluations of governance structure are conducted annually or semiannually as part of a more comprehensive board self-assessment process (see principle 64).

	low	medium	high
1. My board recognizes the importance of structure and intentionally designs it based upon careful analysis, precise criteria, and explicit choices.	1	2	3
2. The organization's governance structure is streamlined and parsimonious.	1	2	3
3. My board's size falls within the range of nine to nineteen members.	no 1		yes 3
4. If your organization has a decentralized governance structure, authority, responsibility, the roles of parent and subsidiary boards are explicitly and precisely specified.	1	2	3
5. If advisory bodies are employed, their functions are clearly specified and differentiated from those of the board.	1	2	3
6. My board has the appropriate number and type of committees needed to support and facilitate its work.	1	2	3
7. The authority of committees vis-à-vis my board is precisely specified; the board governs, committees do governance staff work.	1	2	3
8. Charters (specifying functions and duties) have been formulated for all board committees.	1	2	3

9. Board committees are required to
develop annual work plans.

low	medium	high
1	2	3

10. Governance structure is thoroughly
assessed, and modified if necessary,
on a regular basis.

low	medium	high
1	2	3

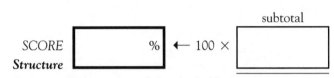

subtotal

SCORE [   ] % ← 100 × [   ]
Structure

the number of items to which you responded multiplied by 3 →

Check-Up 5.1. Structure.

Scoring: Respond only to those items relevant to your board. Count and total your responses, divide the total by 3 times the number of items you answered, and then multiply by 100. The product is your board's percentage of maximum performance in this area.

Getting Started: Structure

- Allocate time at an upcoming board meeting to briefly review your governance structure. Are you employing the principles discussed here?

- Prepare a governance organizational chart, specifying all boards and board committees along with their reporting relationships.

- Review and evaluate the size of your board. Why is your board the size it is? How does the present size facilitate or impair the way, and how well, governance work is performed? Is the present number of members appropriate, or is the board too large or small? Should the size of your board be modified?

- Undertake an initial zero-based committee design activity. Evaluate the need for each committee in terms of helping the board to fulfill its responsibilities and roles, and dealing with critical organizational challenges requiring board input.

• Draft charters for each board committee, specifying key objectives, functions, scope of work, and tasks.

6

Composition

A young student approached the famous director John Houston at a film festival and challenged: "The critics say that fifty percent of the success of your movies is due to nothing but casting." Houston replied: "My young friend, they're wrong; it's all casting."

The story may be apocryphal, but John Houston had a deep appreciation that casting decisions—choosing who plays which parts—is critical to success. So too with governance.

The topic of composition deals with the most foundational aspect of governance: board members, their characteristics, and what they bring to the table. No board can govern above its members' collective capabilities.

Pause for a moment and reflect on your own board's composition—the casting decisions it has made. How were new board members chosen? Was a carefully designed process employed? Were explicit criteria used to seek out, screen, and select members based on organizational challenges and board needs? How many underperforming members does your board have? Who are they? Why are they allowed to continue serving? Which members make the greatest contributions? What distinctive competencies or capacities do they bring to your board?

What are your board's compositional strengths? Think about member characteristics, knowledge, skills, experience, perspectives, and values. Likewise, what are your board's compositional weaknesses, its competency and capacity gaps? Have any members ever been removed for poor performance or a lack of contribution?

Do you know why you were selected as a member of this board? What talents did you bring? Have you fulfilled your promise? Overall, how would you rate the quality of your board's casting?

All boards have a composition model (typically specified in the organization's charter or bylaws). There are three different models:

- *Elected:* Board members are chosen by a vote of the organization's stakeholders. The key here is that stakeholders, or their representatives, directly select board members.

- *Appointed:* Board members are chosen by some other entity; a parent board (in a decentralized governance structure as described in Chapter Five) or a sponsoring organization or governmental agency. Here, control of the board's composition rests outside the organization.

- *Self-selected:* The board nominates and chooses its own members.

These models can be combined in a variety of ways. For example, a board can nominate its own members (self-selected model) but a parent board must approve the slate (appointed model), or some members may be appointed and others elected directly by stakeholder groups.

Although each model imposes different constraints, the elected and appointed options severely restrict a board's ability to determine its own composition. Accordingly, many of the principles presented here are best applied where members are selected by the board itself, or nominated by the board and subject to election or ratification by some other body.

Principle 47

The board proactively designs and manages its composition.

The quality of your board and its ability to govern depend on the characteristics, talents, and experience of members.

It is impossible for your board to design and manage its composition unless it understands its obligations, responsibilities, and roles (the focus of Chapters Three, Four, and Five), along with the key organizational challenges and opportunities with which it must deal. If your board does not know what it is supposed to do, it can't determine the type of individuals needed to do it.

Your board must therefore identify, screen, and select new board members, ensuring their characteristics and competencies are aligned with organizational and board needs. It must then orient new members, specify key expectations for its members, and continuously develop board competencies and capacities. Periodically, it must assess the performance and contributions of individual members. It must also make sure it maintains an appropriate balance between inside, or *ex officio*, and outside members.

Principle 48

Members are recruited and selected on the basis of explicit criteria, employing a profiling process.

Many boards deal with composition issues idiosyncratically and opportunistically. A seat becomes available and an acquaintance of a present member or the CEO is selected, with little investigation of the candidate or board deliberation of the contributions they might make.

Great board casting begins with a carefully designed, criteria-based system that is used to identify, screen, and select new members. Specific criteria will vary—as you can see by the illustrations provided in the box—but the categories should not. We recommend four categories:

- *Foundational qualifications:* Base-line attributes every candidate must possess to be considered for board membership. They should be uniformly applied, with no exceptions. For example, it would not make sense to put an intelligent and otherwise well-qualified person on your board who is unable to attend most meetings.

- *Demographic characteristics:* Dealing with such things as place of residence, community involvement, age, gender, and ethnicity. They are applied as general guidelines to achieve a desired mix of member characteristics.

- *General competencies:* Knowledge, skills, and experience every candidate must possess to become a high-performing and contributing member.

- *Special competencies:* Specific talents needed by your board to address its challenges and opportunities. They are variably applied to select members with different but complementary skill sets and experience; some, not all, board members must possess each of them.

Illustrative New Board Member Screening and Selection Criteria

Note: we are not proposing these criteria as recommendations; they are examples intended to stimulate and focus your board's thinking and deliberation.

FOUNDATIONAL QUALIFICATIONS

- Willingness to serve on the board
- Commitment to and interest in the organization (its vision, mission, and key goals)

- Ability to meet projected time and effort requirements (board and committee meeting preparation and attendance, educational activities, retreats, organizational events)

- High level of personal and professional integrity

DEMOGRAPHIC CHARACTERISTICS

- Percentage of board members that must live or work in the community served

- Minimum and maximum age

- Diversity expectations and targets regarding gender, age, race, and ethnicity

GENERAL COMPETENCIES

- Above average general intelligence

- Ability to clearly articulate ideas and positions

- Capacity to work productively as a member of a deliberative group

- Ability to read, understand, and interpret basic financial statements

SPECIAL COMPETENCIES AND REQUIRED FREQUENCY

- Past experience serving on other boards

- Experience as a senior executive of a roughly similar organization

- Possession of specific expertise (such as labor relations, continuous quality improvement, organizational reengineering, downsizing)

The process of specifying criteria forces your board to be explicit and precise about what it expects of and wants from its new members.

A case-by-case application of criteria can, however, still result in your board lacking the appropriate mix of attributes. Therefore, we recommend this criteria-based approach be employed in conjunction with a board profiling process made up of the following steps:

1. Employ specific foundational, demographic, general, and special competency criteria to construct a profile of your board—that is, a description of its present composition.

2. Use the criteria employed in Step 1 to craft a profile of your board's ideal composition.

3. Compare the actual and ideal profiles to develop a listing of specific member capacities and competencies your board needs in the future.

4. Employ this listing to identify, screen, and select new board members.

Principle 49

New board members participate in a carefully crafted and executed orientation process.

As with any production, good casting isn't enough to guarantee success—the players still have to learn their lines and otherwise figure out what they need to do. That is, if the criteria-based profiling system described here is employed, new members will arrive at the boardroom door with the right stuff, eager to make a contribution. However, a poor orientation process will impair their performance, both immediately and for the long term. The boxed text outlines some of the issues to consider.

Pause and Reflect: Your Orientation

- Did you receive any orientation? Or were you just thrown into the fray?

- How were you oriented to the board?

- Overall, how effective was the orientation in preparing you to become a contributing board member as quickly as possible?
- What were the key strengths and weaknesses of the process?
- What specific things should be done by your board to improve the process?

Unfortunately, most board members are oriented (if at all) in a single, brief meeting with the CEO and board chair. By contrast, a truly effective new member orientation process has the following characteristics:

- Someone (CEO, board chair, a senior board member) is assigned explicit responsibility for managing and overseeing the process.

- The orientation is designed to accomplish specific objectives, such as developing foundational knowledge and skills (what's required to get started, not everything one must know to become a great board member); introducing members to the climate and culture of the organization and board; helping them to feel part of the group; and motivating them to begin participating and contributing.

- It is a process, not a one-time event. We recommend that orientation take place throughout new members' first year of service.

- Multiple approaches are employed, including one-on-one discussions and meetings (with the CEO, other executives, board chair, board committee chairs); tours of facilities, where appropriate; organization-specific written materials; books and articles; in-service programs and briefings; attendance at extramural governance education programs.

- It covers key subject matter, including the nature of the environment in which the organization operates and the characteristics of the most important stakeholder groups. It also familiarizes the new member with the vision, mission, and goals of the organization, and its characteristics: its facilities, structure, management, services, programs, core competencies, competitors, challenges, and relationships with other organizations (suppliers, partners).

- It gives the new member an introduction to the board— its members, committees, mode of operation, culture, bylaws, policies, and work plans—and to the nature of governance obligations, responsibilities, roles, and duties.

- It incorporates mentoring, where the new member is paired with an experienced one. The mentor's role is to serve as a guide, adviser, and coach to the new member during the first year of service. This is one of the most high-leverage orientation strategies.

- The process is periodically assessed and redesigned if necessary.

New members are a precious asset. They must start off on the right foot and be nurtured to achieve their full potential.

Principle 50

The board specifies member expectations.

There's an adage: "You won't get what you don't expect." To be effective, your board must agree upon and communicate its expectations, and members must understand what is expected of them. Your board cannot demand accountability of members absent this.

Some governance consultants recommend drafting a board member job description. We don't, because such statements have a tendency to be wordy, abstract, and imprecise. Rather, your board should simply list its most important expectations of members for *citizenship*, the foundational expectations that are associated with board membership per se, and *performance*, the expectations that must be fulfilled for your board to discharge its obligations and fulfill its responsibilities. The boxed text provides illustrations of these expectations.

Illustrative Board Member Expectations

Citizenship . . . all members are expected to

- Attend 90 percent of regularly scheduled board meetings each year.
- Attend 80 percent of the regularly scheduled meetings of their assigned committees.
- Attend the annual board retreat.
- Fulfill the fiduciary duty of loyalty, putting the interests of stakeholders ahead of their own interests.
- Maintain confidentiality regarding those matters that demand it.
- Do nothing that would discredit the organization.

Performance . . . all members are expected to

- Arrive at board and committee meetings on time and not leave early.
- Serve as a member of at least two standing committees.
- Carefully review background materials contained in the "agenda book" and come to board and committee meetings prepared.
- Actively participate (by sharing ideas, opinions, observations, perspectives, expertise, and experience) in board and committee meeting deliberations and discussions.

- Listen to and respect the opinions and perspectives of other members.

- Be willing to express a dissenting opinion and vote no when the need arises.

- Fully support the board's policies and decisions once they are established.

- Serve as advocates of the organization in their dealings with other organizations, groups, and individuals.

Once formulated, a listing of member expectations can be employed in several ways. First, and most obviously, such a list serves as an explicit reminder and reinforcer of member duties. Second, it can be given to prospective members during the recruitment and selection process to answer a question the best candidates always ask: "What is expected of me if I were to join this board?" Third, it can provide a set of criteria for periodically assessing the performance of individual members (addressed in principle 52).

Principle 51

The board has fixed term lengths and limits the number of terms members can serve.

Term length is the number of years a board member serves before needing to be reappointed. Term limits are the number of successive terms a member can serve before being required to leave the board.

The rationale for term lengths is obvious. Absent them, members would hold their seats in perpetuity. For this reason, most boards have set terms; one to three years is common.

The issue of term limits is more complex and hotly debated. The case against them is based on the argument that performance and contributions need not necessarily decline with length of service or age. Indeed, experience is invaluable. Boards benefit from having seasoned members. Additionally, term limits are totally arbitrary and can result in the loss of talented and dedicated members.

We agree! *However*, even the very best boards generally find it difficult, even impossible, to avoid inviting members back at the conclusion of a term. To do otherwise is perceived as a public firing, which depreciates the member's past service, contributions, and self-worth. If boards had meaningful profiling (principle 48) and member assessment (principle 52) systems in place, and if term renewal was not automatic but based solely on member performance and contributions in addition to organizational and board needs, then term limits would be unnecessary. But this is typically not the case.

Therefore, as a practical measure, we recommend that your board institute term limits. They provide a fail-safe mechanism for ensuring your board's composition is continuously rejuvenated. We recommend two- or three-year terms with a limit of three terms served. After a maximum of six or nine years, a member is required to step down for a minimum of one year before being renominated. Under such an arrangement a board member has adequate time to learn the role and make a contribution, and also the opportunity to assume a leadership position. The term is short enough to guard against member burnout and board stagnation. The only exception to such limits should be an extension of no more than one term (or a portion thereof), if necessary, for a member to assume or complete a term as board chair.

Principle 52

The board periodically assesses the performance and contributions of every member; the results are employed to coach and develop members and make composition redesign decisions.

High-performance boards are characterized by a culture of demonstrated performance, contribution, and accountability. Essential elements for building and maintaining this type of board are member assessment, feedback coupled with coaching that results in an individual development plan, and nonguaranteed term renewal.

Individual member assessment is the third rail of governance — everyone recognizes its importance, but nobody wants to touch it. We estimate that less than 10 percent of boards have such a process in place. To effectively manage its composition, your board must assess the performance and contributions of individual members. This should be done for every board member prior to the conclusion of each term (before any decision about renomination), and based on explicit criteria drawn from your board's specification of member expectations (see principle 50). Either of two methodologies can be employed—self-assessment or 360-degree assessment. In the former, the member responds to a set of questions and reflects upon and assesses personal performance and contributions during the term. In the latter, all members employ a standardized questionnaire to evaluate the individual whose term is ending.

If your board does not have experience in this arena, we recommend beginning with self-assessment; it is not threatening and is reasonably easy to undertake. The boxed text provides some illustrative questions that might be employed.

Illustrative Board Member Self-Assessment Questions

- Do you continue to have the time, energy, and commitment necessary to serve as a productive member of this board?

- Over the long run there must be some balance of what you get by serving on this board and the time and energy you spend as a member. What are the most important benefits you derive from being a member of this board?

- Objectively and candidly, rate your own performance and contributions in comparison to other members—would you place yourself in the lower third, middle third, or upper third?

- What are your most pronounced strengths as a board member?

- What are your most glaring weaknesses?
- What have been your distinctive contributions to this board over the last two years?
- Which board member do you respect the most? What is it about their performance and contribution that you admire?
- What are four or five specific things you must do to become a better member?

Undertaking a 360-degree assessment typically requires outside assistance to design a valid instrument and analyze the data. Additionally, it often causes trepidation on the part of board members—both those being assessed and those doing the assessing. For these reasons, we recommend it be implemented only after your board has become comfortable with self-assessment.

Feedback is the "breakfast of champions" only if it is fed back and employed to improve performance. Irrespective of the method you employ, the insights and data gained from the assessment must be discussed with the member and then used to formulate a plan for change and continued development. Candidly talking with board members about their performance and contributions and working with them to improve both requires some special skills. Ideally, this task should be performed by the board chair; if the chair is unwilling or unable, it could be done by another senior board member. For obvious reasons, this cannot and should not be a task undertaken by the CEO.

Assessment is an effective board composition management tool only if it precipitates change: improvement in a member's performance and contribution—or removal from the board. For the latter to be an option, your board must have an explicit policy that notes (for example):

The ability of our board to make a difference and add value ultimately depends on the dedication, effort, and competencies of individual members. Accordingly, member term renewal is neither automatic nor guaranteed. The decision will be made on a case-by-case basis after a thorough assessment of the member's performance, contributions, and commitment to correct any deficiencies, in addition to board and organizational needs.

Principle 53

Board composition is nonrepresentational.

Of course, boards "represent"—they do so by balancing and aligning the needs, interests, and expectations of various stakeholder groups. The key notion is "balancing and aligning." What individual members must not and cannot do is serve as the representative of a particular interest group or narrow interest.

Consider This

Say you are a member of a board where members all see themselves as representatives of and exclusive advocates for various special interests:

- Harry feels that it is his duty to represent the interest of employees.

- Dan, the only black on the board, perceives himself as an advocate of the African American community.

- Ann sees herself as the standard-bearer for women's issues and rights.

- Stephanie believes that, as a charity, the organization must cut costs to the bone; she views and assesses every issue from this perspective.

- John, who several years ago made the single largest gift the organization had ever received, is only concerned about insuring his own legacy.

> Would this board be able to govern on behalf of all stakeholders? Or would it be torn apart and eventually rendered impotent by divergent interests and perspectives?

A board composed of members who represent any narrow interests will be fragmented by centrifugal forces, as the group described in the boxed text. One board member seeks to advance the interests of and argues on behalf of one group; other members do the same thing from an equally narrow perspective. Board members become advocates and the boardroom takes on the characteristics of a courtroom or legislative chamber. Boards are crippled when members compete with each other by advocating narrow points of view.

Representational governance can take on another face: the belief that a board's composition should mirror the characteristics of stakeholder groups or the community served, for example: 50 percent of the board should be women, 12 percent African American, X percent from the bottom economic quartile (or the top), X percent professionals and X percent blue collar, all members should live and work in the community, or whatever. This approach is problematic for several reasons: First, given the size of most boards (less than twenty members) and the large number of social, demographic, ethnic, economic attributes that would need to be represented, it's impossible to achieve. Second, the primary characteristic of board members must be willingness and ability to govern on behalf of all stakeholders and the community, not whether their collective characteristics perfectly match them.

Don't read the previous paragraph as an argument against the need for and value of diversity—far from it! Diversity of background, experience, and perspective is exceedingly valuable; it's the best safeguard against insular thinking and inappropriate preservation of the status quo. Many boards are too white, too male, too middle-aged, too XXX, and too YYY; they lack the requisite diversity to thrive in the midst of change.

Principle 54

The CEO is a voting *ex officio* member of the board.

Ex officio members arrive at the boardroom door by virtue of another position they hold; they may be either voting or nonvoting. Such members might be executives of the organization, elected government officials, or officers of volunteer groups, to mention only a few examples. *Ex officio* members remain on the board until they vacate the position to which their board seat is linked; they do not have a specified term and are not subject to limits on the number of terms served.

In line with the preceding principle, *ex officio* members, even though they come from a particular group, have the same obligation as any other board member: representing and balancing the interests of all stakeholders.

As addressed in principles 13 and 14, the CEO's relationship with your board and your board's relationship with the CEO is singularly important to the organization's success. It has two aspects: superior-subordinate and partner. The former is reflected in the employment relationship. The board hires, guides and directs, determines the compensation of, and (when the need arises) fires the CEO. The partnership aspect of the relationship is made real and manifested by the CEO's voting board membership. The CEO's obligation to act on behalf of stakeholders in addition to sharing responsibility and authority with the board is reinforced. The CEO is provided with voice inside the boardroom equal to that of other members.

Principle 55

Insiders and those serving *ex officio* comprise less than 25 percent of the board's membership.

Inside board members (whether *ex officio* or not) are employees of the organization or individuals who derive a significant proportion of their livelihood from it.

After a period of time, insiders, no matter how well-intentioned or high-minded, come to think of the organization as either an end in itself or a means to achieve their own professional aspirations. In both cases their focus can become directed inward: on the organization, its success, its growth, its survival per se. Your board's obligation is to make sure the organization advances stakeholder interests. This critical focus could be compromised as the number of insiders increases.

Additionally, with more *ex officio* members (whether insiders or outsiders), the board begins to lose control of its own composition. Membership is determined by decisions made in the past (regarding the type of *ex officio* seats), and the locus of control shifts outside the board itself.

Although the principle "no more than 25 percent insiders and *ex officio* members" is arbitrary, it does strike a balance between your board's need for the expertise insiders and *ex officio* members can bring, the obligation to be stakeholder and externally focused, and the need for your board to control its own composition.

	low	medium	high
1. My board proactively and consciously designs and manages its own composition.	1	2	3
2. New members of my board are recruited and selected on the basis of explicit criteria and as a result of a profiling process.	1	2	3
3. New members of my board participate in a carefully crafted and executed orientation process.	1	2	3
4. My board specifies member expectations.	1	2	3

(continued)

	low	medium	high
5. My board has fixed term lengths and limits the number of terms members can serve.	1	2	3
6. My board periodically assesses the performance of every member and employs the results to coach and develop them and make composition redesign decisions.	1	2	3

	no	somewhat	yes
7. The composition of my board is representational.	3	2	1

	no		yes
8. The CEO is a voting, *ex officio* member of my board.	1		3
9. Insiders and those serving *ex officio* comprise less than 25 percent of the members of my board.	1		3

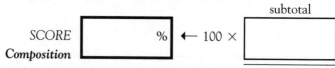

SCORE
Composition [   ] % ←— 100 × [   ] subtotal

the number of items to which you responded multiplied by 3 —→

Check-Up 6.1. Composition.

Scoring: Respond only to those items relevant to your board. Count and total your responses, divide the total by 3 times the number of items you answered, and then multiply by 100. The product is your board's percentage of maximum performance in this area.

Getting Started: Composition

• At an upcoming meeting, conduct a discussion of how, and how well, your board manages its composition. You might want to address the questions about casting at the beginning of this chapter, and the ones in the box on orientation.

- Develop a set of initial new board member selection criteria—foundational qualifications, demographic characteristics, general competencies, and special competencies.

- Assign a board committee the task of assessing and then developing objectives for a new member orientation process.

- Devote some time at an upcoming meeting to identifying your most important member expectations.

- If your board does not have fixed term lengths and limitations on the number of terms that can be served, debate the pros and cons of implementing them.

- If your board does not periodically assess the performance and contributions of individual members, design and implement a simple process for doing so. Consider using the box titled "Illustrative Board Member Self-Assessment Questions" to construct a tool.

- If the CEO is not a voting member of your board, spend some time debating the pros and cons of giving the position an *ex officio* voting board seat.

7

Infrastructure

Boards are among an organization's most important components but, typically, are among the least well endowed in terms of the infrastructure that is in place to support their work. Management and operations require the right amount and mix of resources, and so does governance.

Infrastructure refers to the resources and systems necessary for the performance of governance work. The right infrastructure is essential in that it increases the effectiveness and efficiency of the board's most valuable and scarcest asset: its own attention, time, and effort.

Principle 56

The board has its own budget.

Few boards have their own budget, but this is an excellent practice for several reasons. First, your board should subject itself to the same financial discipline it expects of the organization. Second, budgeting provides your board an opportunity to plan for the resources it needs. Third, having a budget eliminates the necessity of requesting funds from management on an item-by-item basis. Fourth, a separate allocation of funds and recording of expenditures accounts for the true costs of governance.

Led by the chair, the executive committee should prepare a draft budget at the beginning of each fiscal year which is then discussed and approved by the full board. Several broad categories of expenditures can be budgeted:

- *Personnel:* proportions of salaries and benefits of personnel who provide staff and secretarial support to the board

- *Services:* board consultation, governance-specific legal assistance, directors' and officers' liability insurance

- *Operations:* supplies, telephone, duplication and printing, postage and mailing, food service (at meetings), reimbursed member meeting attendance expenses

- *Education and development:* materials, books, subscriptions, memberships, member participation in educational conferences, and fees and expenses associated with conducting periodic board retreats

Principle 57

The board has adequate staff support.

The proper amount and type of staff support are critical elements of infrastructure. Most boards are typically staffed, as one of many duties, by the CEO's assistant or secretary—who is usually among the most overworked employees in the organization. As a consequence, board support gets squeezed or moved to a back burner by other things that demand attention. A person (executive assistant or secretary) should be assigned the function of board coordinator, assuming responsibility for providing and directing governance staff support. A specific proportion of the person's time and effort should be allocated to performing this role and reflected in your board's budget. Additionally, the board coordinator function should have an explicit job description like the one illustrated in the boxed text.

Illustrative Board Coordinator Function Description

PURPOSE

The board requires adequate staff support to optimize its performance. To provide this support, a person will be assigned to perform the function of board coordinator.

POSITION

The person performing this function is [name], presently occupying the position of [job title]. It is estimated that XX percent of this person's time will be devoted to governance staffing. For administrative purposes, this person reports to the CEO; in fulfilling the tasks described here the board coordinator functions under the direction of the CEO and board chair.

KEY TASKS

- Preparing agendas and supporting materials for board and committee meetings

- Compiling and distributing materials (agenda books) for all board and committee meetings

- Taking minutes at board and committee meetings

- Maintaining all board records

- Maintaining a file of board policies and decisions

- Ensuring that analyses, reports, and other materials requested by the board are prepared

- Serving as the point of first contact for board member requests

- Handling preparations for board educational sessions and retreats

- Handling all board-related correspondence

- Performing other duties as requested by the CEO, chair, and their designees to support effective and efficient board functioning

Principle 58

The board formulates annual objectives.

The development of annual objectives is an important tool for planning, focusing, and organizing your board's work. At the beginning of each year, the executive committee should specify the most important things your board must accomplish. The committee's draft objectives should then be discussed, modified if necessary, and approved by your board. The question is: What must our board achieve in order to meet its obligations and fulfill its responsibilities during the forthcoming year? The boxed text provides some illustrations.

Illustrative Board Objectives

By the end of this year our board will

- Develop and implement a plan to increase board member involvement in key community groups and improve their input to our governance process.

- Identify key organizational stakeholders and begin the process of understanding what they want from and expect of the organization.

- Review and if necessary redraft the organization's vision statement, increasing its specificity regarding core purposes and values.

- Craft a CEO succession plan.

- Commission management to undertake a comprehensive study of consumer satisfaction with the quality of the organization's services.

- Conduct an assessment of the extent our board is fulfilling its responsibilities and roles, and employ the results to engage in action planning to improve governance performance and contributions.

- Hold a retreat focused on visioning, goal specification, and the board's involvement in strategic planning.

- Have at least five members of the board, accompanied by the CEO, participate in the XZY Governance Conference.

- Develop charters and annual objectives for all board standing committees.

Carefully conceived, explicit, and precise board objectives, developed annually, provide the basis for developing agendas and managing meetings (principles 59 and 60), formulating committee charges and work plans (principle 45), designing education and development activities (principles 62 and 63), and board assessment (principle 64).

Principle 59

Meeting agendas are carefully devised plans for deploying the board's attention and time.

Your board exists, in both a legal and functional sense, only when it meets—"between raps of the gavel." Board meetings are the center of governance; they are where the work gets done. Both the way they are planned and conducted and the dynamics that emerge in them significantly affect governance quality. Meetings must be designed to stimulate and focus the attention, energy, and competencies of board members. High-performance governance begins with your board's controlling and optimizing the use of its meeting time. The key to doing this is agenda planning.

Most agenda items flow from three sources: management proposals, the annual board objectives, and committee work products. The executive committee should convene (either face to face or by telephone conference call) several weeks prior to each board meeting to set the agenda based on these inputs, deciding which items should be scheduled and for each the objective sought; how much time will be allocated; and the type of background material needed to prepare board members to address it.

Board meeting time is a precious resource; craft a plan for effectively and efficiently allocating it. We recommend the format displayed in the "Illustrative Agenda Format" box.

Illustrative Agenda Format

Place: Conference room A

Date: Wednesday March 15, 200X

Start time: 5:00 P.M.

End time: 8:30 P.M.

Please confirm your attendance by calling Ms. Howell at XXX-XXXX.

Item #1   • Reflection; role of the board as an advocate for the disadvantaged and underserved in our area

Time allocated: • 5:00 P.M. to 5:10 P.M.

Presenter: • Ms. Hammel (Chair)

Background materials: • Executive summary of Community Needs Assessment Survey; agenda book, Tab A

Item #2   • Approvals
                     Board meeting minutes of 2/14/0X
                     Designated state provider certification
                     State license, final report (previously discussed in draft form at meeting of 1/12/0X
                     Employee service award recognitions

Time allocated: • 5:10 P.M. to 5:15 P.M.

Objective: • Consent

Presenter: • Ms. Hammel (Chair)

Background materials: • Agenda book, Tab B

ENDS

<u>Item #3</u>	• Provision of services to the disadvantaged
Time allocated:	• 5:15 P.M. to 5:30 P.M.
Objective:	• Policy formulation
Presenter:	• Mr. Jacobs (Chair, vision and goals committee)
Background materials:	• Draft policy alternatives and recommendations; agenda book, Tab C

MANAGEMENT

<u>Item #4</u>	• Executive's report
Time allocated:	• 5:30 P.M. to 5:50 P.M.
Objective:	• Information; Q and A
Presenter:	• Mr. Samuelson (CEO)
Background materials:	• Audio tape included with agenda book
<u>Item #5</u>	• Revised employment contract and severance agreement
Time allocated:	• 5:50 P.M. to 6:10 P.M.
Objective:	• Decision
Presenter:	• Mr. Benson (Chair, executive performance and compensation committee)
Background materials:	• Agenda book, Tab C

QUALITY

<u>Item #6</u>	• Client satisfaction survey results
Time allocated:	• 6:10 P.M. to 6:30 P.M.
Objective:	• Information
Presenter:	• Mr. Hauerman (Chair, quality committee)
Background materials:	• Agenda book, Tab D

Item #7	• Revised quality indicators and standards
Time allocated:	• 6:30 P.M. to 6:50 P.M.
Objective:	• Policy and oversight
Presenter:	• Mr. Hauerman (Chair, quality committee)
Background materials:	• Agenda book, Tab E

FINANCE

Item #8	• Auditor's report
Time allocated:	• 6:50 P.M. to 7:30 P.M.
Objective:	• Oversight
Presenter:	• Mr. Williams (Partner; Collen, Powell and Hovell, CPAs)
Background materials:	• Executive summary included in agenda book, Tab F; full report provided as separate attachment
Item #9	• Executive session with audit partner
Time allocated:	• 7:30 P.M. to 8:00 P.M.
Objective:	• Oversight
Presenters:	• Ms. Hammel (Chair) and Mr. Williams (Partner; Collen, Powell and Hovell, CPAs)
Background materials:	• Same as agenda item #7

GOVERNANCE

Item #10	• Nomination of Mr. Jacob Nester as a new member of the board
Time allocated:	• 8:00 P.M. to 8:15 P.M.
Objective:	• Decision
Presenter:	• Ms. Kraus (Chair, governance committee)
Background materials:	• Résumé and committee assessment; agenda book, Tab G

Item #11	• Meeting assessment
Time allocated:	• 8:15 P.M. to 8:30 P.M.
Objective:	• Oversight
Presenter:	• Ms. Hammel (Chair)
Background	
materials:	• None

Note: After the meeting concludes a reception and dinner will be held at Nathan's Restaurant to welcome Mr. Jon Andrews, the newly appointed chief operating officer. Confirm your attendance by calling Ms. Howell at XXX-XXXX. Please make every effort to join us.

Meetings should not be held concurrently with meals, as this wastes time and diverts attention. Breaking bread together can be a very useful communal experience and catalyst, but such activities should be held before or after meetings or as separately scheduled events.

Without exception, meetings should begin and conclude on time. The starting and ending times noted on the agenda should never be violated. This conveys an attitude of seriousness and efficiency, in addition to respecting the value of members' time. In all but the most unusual circumstances, meetings should not be scheduled to last more than three hours. Member attention and energy levels begin to deteriorate after this period of time.

Most boards make the mistake of overestimating the number of items that can be thoughtfully discussed, deliberated, and acted upon. (Recall how many times in the past several years your board did not get through the agenda or had to meet longer than planned.) Here, less is generally better: place fewer, rather than more, items on the agenda. Consider the following questions when evaluating potential agenda items: Why should the board be dealing with this issue? Is it critical to our board's fulfilling its obligations and responsibilities? Is this a matter on which the board must weigh in and can add substantial value? A proposed item should be automatically rejected unless the strongest case can be made for including it.

For each agenda item, the type of issue and its objective should be noted. The type of issues that come before your board can deal with policy, decision making, or oversight regarding ends, management, quality, finances, or board operations. Classifying each agenda item in this way reinforces your board's responsibilities and roles. Each item should have an explicit objective that fits one of four possibilities:

- *Consent* items—routine housekeeping matters that need neither discussion nor deliberation, but still require board approval. They are grouped together as a single agenda item. Members review these materials prior to the meeting and, if no one has any questions or concerns, the entire block is approved with a single vote and no discussion. This can free up a significant amount of time that might otherwise be squandered on minor issues. Any member can request that an item be discussed and voted upon separately.

- *Information* items—matters the board needs to know about, but for which no discussion or action is needed. The flow is one way, from the presenter to the board; however, questions and requests for clarification are entertained.

- *Discussion* items—issues the board talks about and provides input on; an exchange takes place but no action is necessary.

- *Action* items—issues that require discussion, deliberation, and a board vote.

A precise amount of time should be allocated to each item. Again, it pays to be a bit liberal here; overestimating the time needed to address an issue causes fewer problems than underestimating. If more time is needed to handle an item, a decision should be made on the spot by the chair regarding what else on the agenda should receive less time or be tabled. This process, when employed consistently, disciplines your board in setting priorities and using its time efficiently.

Each item should have an individual assigned to make a presentation, answer questions, and facilitate the discussion. Resource materials supporting each item, if needed, should be identified and included as attachments in the agenda book. Include only those materials necessary to help members understand an issue, ask questions, and engage in a thoughtful discussion. Some briefing materials cannot be effectively and efficiently conveyed in writing (or they take too much effort to prepare). When greater richness is required, consider preparing an audiotape to supplement written materials and include it with the agenda package. Agenda books should be distributed to board members about a week preceding the meeting so as to provide enough time for review—but not so much that they wind up at the bottom of members' to-do pile.

The same agenda planning and management system should be employed by all of your board's committees.

Principle 60

Board meetings are managed and conducted to promote high levels of effectiveness, efficiency, and creativity.

We've all experienced them, far too often: mind-numbing, deenergizing, unfocused meetings that accomplish little and waste members' time. Whether your board meetings are productive depends on, in addition to agenda planning, how well they are facilitated. Here are a few recommendations:

Begin with some type of brief activity that reinforces your board's obligation and responsibilities. One of the best illustrations of this practice we've seen occurred on a Catholic hospital board on which one of us sat. The chair began each meeting by making an observation or posing a question dealing with some "big picture" aspect of governance typically related to an important agenda item. She would then ask members to share their reflections. The board looked forward to these discussions. They helped members get into a frame of mind that transcended the detail and focused their attention on obligations, responsibilities, and roles.

Never back up and summarize what has transpired for members arriving late. This rewards tardiness and wastes the time of those who were prompt. Also, do not spend meeting time re-presenting or summarizing information previously forwarded in the agenda book; expect and assume it has been read and digested. Meeting time can then be spent responding to questions and discussing possible action.

We will deal with the broader aspects of board leadership in principle 61. However, first and foremost, the chair must either possess or be willing and able to quickly acquire the knowledge and skills necessary to run productive meetings. Since facilitation skills significantly influence meeting effectiveness, efficiency, and creativity, incumbents should be required to develop them. There are a number of continuing education programs and workshops offered by colleges, professional and trade associations, and governance support organizations (such as the National Center for Nonprofit Boards), plus many excellent books on the subject. (See the boxed text for a sampling of these books.) The chair should also take advantage of informal tutoring by board members, staff members, or other individuals who are skilled in this area.

Running Better Meetings

Here are some resources that can help prospective and current chairs develop the necessary knowledge and skills:

- Richard Chang, *Meetings That Work*
- Charles Hawkins, *First-Aid for Meetings*

- George Kieffer, *The Strategy of Meetings*

- Milo Frank, *How to Run Successful Meetings in Half the Time*

- Michael Doyle, *How to Make Meetings Work*

Every effort should be made to maximize that amount of meeting time members spend interacting with each other, rather than passively listening. Talk is the way your board accomplishes its work. We've found that far too much precious meeting time is spent conveying information better presented in other ways.

Listening and Talking

How much of your board meeting time is spent passively listening (to background materials, briefings, committee reports) as compared to actively interacting—that is, members talking with one another, discussing, questioning, deliberating, weighing alternatives? The ratio for most boards is about 60:40. Although clearly extreme, consider a board that spends all of its time, every moment of every meeting, just listening. Could it really govern? The answer: obviously not. There would be no discussion, no questions, no deliberation, no weighing of alternatives, no interchange of ideas, no debate—none of the work necessary for acting, formulating policy, making decisions, and overseeing.

Often, in handling specific agenda items, a board's process is haphazard because members are not in sync: an issue is presented, several members express their preferred solutions, a few others ask for clarification regarding alternatives, someone questions whether the board should even be dealing with the matter at all, and so on. To be effective, your board must focus its attention and be together when doing so. In considering a given agenda item, we recommend that members move through the following steps in sequence, together:

1. Develop a full understanding of the issue, problem, or opportunity and precisely define it.
2. Clarify assumptions.
3. Specify alternative solutions and choices.
4. Weigh and assess alternatives
5. Make a choice—formulate a policy or make a decision.
6. Determine follow-up activities required, if any.

If your board conducts its meetings using *Robert's Rules of Order*, consider discontinuing the practice. First developed in the mid-1800s, these procedures were designed to manage deliberation and decision making by very large legislative bodies (initially the English Parliament). This highly structured and rigid process is inappropriate and unnecessarily cumbersome for small groups such as boards. It generally saps their creativity and impedes rather than facilitates the effectiveness and efficiency of their meetings.

Most board minutes resemble a transcript, attempting to capture the flow of discussion taking place in a meeting. Compiled in this way they require huge amounts of effort to produce and result in documents that are largely symbolic, having little substantive value. Rather than taking traditional minutes, we recommend using the form portrayed in Figure 7.1 to summarize each agenda item.

In addition to noting the type of item and objective, the recommended format summarizes key discussion points as a brief bulleted list, mentions background materials included in the agenda book, and describes the follow-up required, if any. Attached to the form, where appropriate, is the policy or decision summary form (discussed in Chapter Four and portrayed as Figures 4.2 and 4.3).

Allocate about ten minutes at the end of each meeting for evaluating how well your board planned for and used its time. The

Agenda Item Summary Form

Meeting date: _____

Item number: _____

Type: ☐ consent   Objective: ☐ information

☐ ends   ☐ discussion

☐ management   ☐ action/policy

☐ quality   ☐ action/decision

☐ finances   ☐ action/oversight

☐ self

Key discussion point summary:

Decision or policy summary form attached: ☐

Background materials included in the agenda book:

Follow-up required:

Figure 7.1. Board Meeting Minutes Format.

boxed text presents some questions that can be posed and discussed in this context. When your board first starts to do this, expect resistance; with time and persistence the effort will bear fruit.

Board Meeting Evaluation Questions

- Did the agenda book contain useful information in the right form that genuinely helped members understand the issues? What should be done differently?

- Did every member come to the meeting fully prepared?

- Did the agenda focus on important issues—those demanding board attention where real value can be added? What agenda items should have been eliminated?

- What proportion of board meeting time was spent talking versus listening? What can be done to increase the percentage?

- Did members have ample opportunity to ask questions and express their opinions?

- Was the meeting effective, efficient, and creative?

- What specific member behaviors were most helpful? What behaviors were deleterious?

- How effective was the chair's facilitation of the meeting? What might have been done better or differently?

Principle 61

The chair is carefully selected, understands the role, and is able to perform it effectively.

A great chair does not guarantee a high level of board performance, but a poor one always undermines it.

The chair must be able to perform four roles:

- *Ceremonial and representational:* symbolizing and personifying both the organization and board. The chair is often called upon to be a spokesperson to both external constituents and internal audiences.

- *Leadership:* the key aspect of which is influencing, motivating, organizing, focusing, and monitoring the board and the way it goes about its work.

- *Facilitative:* planning and conducting effective, efficient, and creative board meetings (separately addressed in principle 60).

- *Consultative:* serving as a confidant and adviser to the CEO on organizational and governance issues and executive-board relationships.

The board chair should be selected with great care, based on ability to perform the multiple roles required of the job. The position should not be a reward for long tenure or past contributions, nor should it be bestowed on a member because of status or availability.

The CEO should be a member of the board (as noted in principle 54), but should not serve as chair for several reasons: First, when the CEO is also the board chair, the already fuzzy line that differentiates management and governance work is further blurred. Confusion and conflict regarding authority and responsibilities often result. Second, this dual role concentrates too much power in the hands of one person. The CEO, already possessing considerable influence due to full-time presence and access to information and the organization's resources, can totally dominate a board. Boards serve as stakeholders' checks and balances within the organization; the scale is tipped when the CEO is also the chair.

The term of chairs in most nonprofit organizations is one year; we recommend two. This provides an adequate amount of time to get comfortable with the role and make a contribution.

Typically, the vice chair moves into the position of chair. This provides an opportunity for an incumbent to have time to develop the necessary knowledge and skills to discharge the position effectively. However, we feel it unwise to establish a series of positions a person automatically moves through to become chair (say, treasurer to secretary to vice chair to chair). This practice locks a board into a succession arrangement where the chair is actually selected many years in advance. This can be a problem, as opportunities and board needs change.

Selection of the chair and execution of the position's duties should be guided by a job description. (See Resource D for an illustration.) This provides a way to hold a chair accountable in addition to facilitating the orientation, development, and evaluation of a new incumbent.

Principle 62

The board is serious about continuous member development and has a plan for accomplishing it.

No board member possesses all the knowledge and skills needed when entering the boardroom for the first time. In addition, new issues constantly emerge and organizational challenges and opportunities as well as board needs change over time. Thus continuous education of members and development of the board is essential. This begins with new member orientation (principle 49).

The quality of board work is simultaneously the result of and constrained by the board's collective knowledge and skills. Your board must have a plan to enhance its capacities supported by a budget for doing so (see principle 56). Here are some key elements:

• Conduct periodic board retreats. We feel this is so important it is addressed separately as principle 63.

- Include several articles on emerging trends and issues in each board agenda book and allocate time at board meetings to briefly discuss them. This practice reinforces the importance of continual learning and provides an efficient way for doing so. Management staff and board members should constantly be on the lookout for suitable materials.

- Enter subscriptions for all board members to key magazines and newsletters dealing with both substantive (industry, market, organizational) and governance issues.

- Two or three times a year, distribute a carefully selected book on governance to board members.

- Have management (with guidance and direction supplied by the executive or governance committees) prepare briefing books on important issues and matters that will be coming before the board. This is one of the most effective development strategies because it is targeted; necessity always provides the most powerful motivation to learn.

- On a rotating basis, send small groups of members to governance-related conferences, seminars, and workshops. This practice provides members an opportunity to be exposed to a broad range of ideas and issues.

Principle 63

The board holds periodic retreats.

Retreats (some, not liking the negative military connotation, call them *advances*) provide a unique opportunity for board education, facilitated discussion, and a focused forum for addressing issues not possible at board meetings. Annual or semiannual retreats can help your board prepare for the future, grow, change, rejuvenate itself, and become more effective.

We facilitate over sixty board retreats a year, and have developed a number of recommendations for designing and conducting really great ones. Assign the responsibility for retreat planning to your board's executive or governance committee. This should be an ongoing activity throughout the year, not something done at the last moment, and the retreat itself should be scheduled far in advance. We recommend at least six months. This is the best way to ensure a high level of attendance. Little is gained by holding a retreat when only a portion of the board is present.

Select a specific objective, theme, or issue that will serve as the retreat's focus. Make sure it's something that cannot be effectively addressed at regularly scheduled meetings. "Retreating" to conduct routine business is a waste of time and money. Most retreat topics fall into the following categories:

- General education and development

- Reviewing and analyzing results of a board assessment and engaging in action planning to improve performance and contributions (see principle 64)

- Developing annual board objectives and a work plan

- Board team building

- Gaining a better understanding of industry or market trends, competitors, and partners, and discussing their consequences and implications

- Building more effective relationships between the board and management

- Addressing significant "over the horizon" organizational challenges and opportunities

The term *retreat* connotes a withdrawal from the overpacked and harried day-to-day work environment to a less frantic and distracting place where people can relax, focus their attention, and release their creativity. Take the opportunity to get out of town. The venue need not be far away or expensive.

Retreats give the organization's leaders (board, management, and other attendees) a chance to interact in ways difficult to do back home; encourage and facilitate this. For example, plan all meals as communal events; this maximizes inclusion and interaction. Seize the opportunity to celebrate organizational and board accomplishments.

Consider retaining the services of an experienced consultant to facilitate the retreat; make these arrangements well in advance. The best talent is in great demand. Facilitator quality, more than any other factor, will determine your retreat's success. Request references and talk with past clients. The most effective facilitators are entertaining experts, combining broad and in-depth expertise and experience with the ability to convey ideas in an engaging, powerful, and stimulating way.

Allocate at least 50 percent of the retreat meeting time to discussion. Just sitting and listening to speakers (no matter how talented) is deadly and squanders a tremendous opportunity for enlightened engagement around key issues. Instead, ensure there is an action planning component. The board must walk away with a precise notion of what comes next. Retreats that do not precipitate some form of follow-up action are a waste of effort.

Retreats can be expensive; work from a budget. In addition, formally evaluate all aspects of the retreat. Incorporate this evaluation into planning next year's event.

Principle 64

The board engages in a periodic self-assessment and formulates action plans to improve its performance and contributions.

Assessment, feedback, analysis, and action planning form the "breakfast of champions." Individual board member assessment was addressed in principle 52; we turn here to evaluating the board as a whole.

By design or default, boards continually assess themselves. But unless these perceptions are systematically collected, organized, shared, analyzed, and acted upon, they will not improve governance. Accordingly, your board should engage in a periodic assessment (we recommend every other year) of those things that most affect its performance and contributions: how well your board discharges its responsibility for ends, executive performance, quality, and finances; and the appropriateness of its structure, composition, and infrastructure.

A questionnaire, whether custom-designed or obtained from an outside source, should be used to gather members' perceptions. Self-assessments are relatively easy to conduct, inexpensive, and do not require a great deal of time to administer.

However, self-assessment per se, no matter how well done, never improves performance. The information collected must be fed back to—and analyzed and discussed by—your board. Using the results, your board must then develop specific action plans for improving how it governs. We recommend that these activities take place at a special board meeting or retreat.

---

1. My board has its own budget and is appropriately funded.

   low medium high
   1   2   3

2. My board has adequate staff support.

   low medium high
   1   2   3

3. My board formulates annual objectives.   low   medium   high
                                              1   2   3

4. My board's meeting agendas are carefully low   medium   high
   planned.   1   2   3

5. My board's meetings are well managed   low   medium   high
   and facilitated; they are effective,   1   2   3
   efficient, and creative.

6. The chair is carefully selected, under-   low   medium   high
   stands the role, and is able to perform   1   2   3
   it effectively.

7. My board is serious about continual   low   medium   high
   member development and has a plan   1   2   3
   to accomplish it.

8. My board holds periodic retreats.   low   medium   high
                                              1   2   3

9. My board periodically assesses its   low   medium   high
   performance and contributions and,   1   2   3
   employing the results, engages in
   action planning to improve
   governance quality.

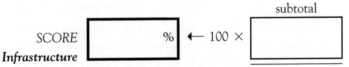

subtotal

SCORE [   ] % ← 100 × [   ]

Infrastructure

the number of items to which you responded multiplied by 3 →

Check-Up 7.1. Infrastructure.

Scoring: Respond only to those items relevant to your board. Count and total your responses, divide the total by 3 times the number of items you answered, and then multiply by 100. The product is your board's percentage of maximum performance in this area.

Getting Started: Infrastructure

- Conduct an audit of your board's infrastructure. How adequate is it? Does your board have the appropriate mix of resources it needs to govern effectively and efficiently? What is missing? What elements of infrastructure must be put in place to optimize your board's performance and contributions?

- Allocate some time at an upcoming meeting to discussing and then sketching out about a half-dozen of the most important objectives your board must accomplish over the next year. Develop some initial work plans; specify the tasks committees must perform to help the board accomplish these objectives.

- Have a frank discussion about the effectiveness, efficiency, and creativity of your board's meetings. What are the positives and negatives? Consider implementing some of the recommendations presented here: agenda planning, agenda format, policy and decision-making summary forms, not using *Robert's Rules of Order*, and revising the minute-taking process.

- Analyze the quality of your board's leadership: the chair position in general and its present occupant. This is tough to do in a meeting. Therefore we suggest that all members be asked to respond anonymously, in writing. The responses should be collated, organized, and discussed by executive committee. Based on this, a list of leadership issues should be prepared and submitted to the board for discussion. Here are some useful questions for members to consider:

  What are the most pronounced strengths of the board chair?

What are the most glaring weaknesses of the board chair?

What specific things should the chair do, stop doing, and do better to lead more effectively?

How could the position of board chair be strengthened?

- At a meeting, pose these questions:

  How serious is our board about continual member development?

  What important knowledge, skills, and perspectives are we lacking?

  What suggestions in principles 62 and 63 should be implemented to develop the capacities of our board?

- If your board doesn't undertake a periodic self-assessment, or does it poorly, consider employing some of the items in the check-ups in this book to design an inventory; have members complete it, then feed back a summary and conduct a mini-retreat to analyze the data and do some targeted action planning.

8

Transforming Your Board

The first seven chapters have dealt with what your board must do to improve its performance and contribution. This chapter focuses on how to go about it—the transformational process. This transformation has five components:

- Understanding the principles of benchmark governance

- Assessing your board in light of these principles

- Formulating a set of principles, tailored to your board, that specifies how it will govern

- Undertaking transformational work as a team

- Being aware of the challenges associated with mounting and sustaining significant change efforts

Characteristics of Benchmark Governance

Significant change begins with a vivid and empowering image of what your board and its process of governing should be like, at its very best. By getting to this point in the book, you're there. You understand the principles of governing regarding nonprofit organization board obligations, responsibilities, roles, structure, composition, and infrastructure. These principles provide your board with an ideal target to head toward.

Of course, understanding in this area can always be taken further. This book gives you a good view of the target, but there's much more information available. For additional readings, both in published materials and online, see the listing in Resource F.

Assessment

To move toward a goal you need to know your current location — a navigational fix. By completing the check-ups in the first seven chapters, you have already done most of the work. All that remains is bringing everything together in one place and doing some analysis and reflection. Check-Up 8.1 provides a convenient score sheet.

---

1. Enter scores for the *check-ups* in the appropriate boxes:

   Basics (from Chapter One, page 6)   ☐

   Obligations (from Chapter Two, page 20)   ☐

   Ends responsibility (from Chapter Three, page 30)   ☐

   Management responsibility (from Chapter Three,   ☐
       page 40)

   Quality responsibility (from Chapter Three,   ☐
       page 47)

   Finances responsibility (from Chapter Three,   ☐
       page 54)

   Role performance (from Chapter Four, page 76)   ☐

   Structure (from Chapter Five, page 95)   ☐

   Composition (from Chapter Six, page 114)   ☐

   Infrastructure (from Chapter Seven, page 139)   ☐

Sum of all scores:

Summary score (sum of all scores divided by 10):

2. Using the detail scores recorded in Step 1, place a dot on each of the associated axes of the practice profile chart, then connect them to form a "spider diagram."

Check-Up 8.1. Putting Things Together.

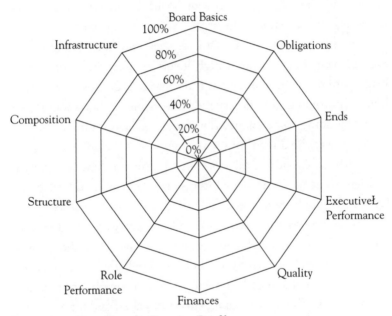

Figure 8.1. Your Board's Practice Profile.

The *summary score* is an indicator of your board's overall fitness. Above 80 percent is high-performance; between 80 percent and 60 percent is adequate; below 60 percent is problematic (and we'd regard anything under 40 percent as impaired).

The spider diagram accompanying the check-up (Figure 8.1) is a graphical profile of your board across the dimensions of governance that most affect its performance and contributions. Before you form any conclusions, step back and consider how realistic the diagram is, both for strengths and for weaknesses.

For those dimensions rated above 80 percent, was your initial assessment candid and accurate? Look over the check-ups that produced high scores. Review each of the individual items and your responses to them. Most self-assessments suffer from a *halo effect*— a tendency for ratings to reflect the overall value of the institution rather than its actual varying strengths and weaknesses. Take a deep breath and be really tough on your board. Change your ratings as necessary and recompute the scores where appropriate.

Which of your board's characteristics and practices are truly high-performance? To build high levels of spirit and motivation, your board must recognize what it does well. Additionally, areas of high performance can deteriorate over time. What should your board be doing to celebrate, reinforce, and maintain excellence?

Do any of the dimensions with high scores include problem areas? Although your overall score on a particular dimension might be high, some of its individual items may have merited low scores. Do not overlook them. These are weeds in a patch of roses.

Those dimensions rated below 60 percent warrant careful attention. They are your board's weaknesses, but offer the greatest transformational opportunities. Look through the check-ups and identify the specific board characteristics and governance practices rated low. List them on separate sheets of paper, and for each one, answer the following questions:

1. What, specifically, does your board do (or not do) that is problematic? Describe the characteristic or governance practice in general terms and jot down some specific examples.

2. What are the consequences? How does this characteristic or practice impair your board's performance and contributions?

What are the implications?

3. Why does your board have this characteristic or engage in this practice? What are the reasons for it?

4. How difficult would it be to change? What are the primary barriers to doing so?

Select about a half-dozen of the lowest-rated characteristics and practices you've identified—those that have the most significant impact on your board's performance and contributions, and the ones that appear to be most changeable. For each, work through the following questions to rough out an initial action plan:

1. What is the objective? That is: What would this particular characteristic or practice look like if it were truly high-performance?

2. What specific things must be done to transform this problematic characteristic or practice into a high-performance one? Be concrete and precise; note the actions, tasks, and activities that would be necessary.

3. What process should be undertaken to ensure success? What are the required steps and their sequence? For example: general discussion of the problematic characteristic or practice with the full board; assignment to a committee for analysis and recommendations; review by legal counsel; full board discussion, deliberation, vote, and (if passed) bylaw modification.

4. What barriers and problems might arise? How can they be eliminated, reduced, or resolved?

5. How will you know that success has been achieved?

6. What must be done to make sure that the change sticks?

Principle-Based Governance Practice

Assessment and action planning can identify and begin to address specific problems that compromise your board's performance and contributions. But over the long run, to be high-performance, your board's governance practice must be based on and driven by a set of principles. Such principles will focus your board's precious and very limited attention, time, and energy. When continuously and consistently applied, they will guide the way your board meets its obligations, fulfills its responsibilities, performs its roles, designs its structure, crafts its composition, and builds its infrastructure.

Start thinking about the specific principles your board should formulate and adopt. Review the sixty-four principles and associated practices of high-performance governance presented in this book (consolidated as Resource A). Which ones does your board presently employ (even though it may not recognize or formally codify them)? Which ones are not employed? Why?

Identify a half-dozen principles that, if adopted, would have the greatest impact on improving your board's performance and contributions. Draft a handful of principles for your board. You'll find some useful illustrations in Resource E.

Team Work

All organizational change begins in the mind, heart, and soul of a single individual. But for change to be initiated, take hold, and have an impact, understanding and action must be expanded from you to your board as a whole. This section presents some recommendations for getting started.

Suggest that copies of this book be made available to, and read by, all board members. Your board must have a collective understanding of principle-based governance in addition to the specific principles that constitute high-performance governance practice.

Devote a portion of a board meeting to discussing the ideas presented here and how they might be adopted by your board to improve its performance and contributions. Talk frankly about the costs and benefits of implementing a principle-based approach in whole or part. Take a vote on whether or not to move ahead.

Have all members complete the check-ups, compile the responses, calculate average scores for each individual item and dimension, then produce a composite "board as a whole" spider diagram.

Form an ad hoc committee to review the assessment results and begin drafting an initial set of governing principles for your board. We recommend developing no more than about twenty of them that focus on specific practices identified as most problematic and potentially transforming. Circulate the draft principles to board members and solicit their feedback.

Hold a board retreat to review assessment results, discuss and deliberate draft principles, and develop action plans for implementing each principle. (The boxed text provides an illustration of what you should be looking for.) Codify the principles and circulate them to all board members.

Principle-Based Governance Action Planning

Principle:

Our board will guide and direct the organization on behalf of its stakeholders primarily through the formulation of policies regarding ends, executive performance, quality, finances, and governance. Where feasible and practical, action items and recommendations coming before the board for discussion and vote shall be framed as draft policies. Board policies will be codified and distributed employing a form specifically designed for this purpose. All board policies will be reviewed annually.

Action planning elements:

- CEO, board chair, and governance committee chair to read *Reinventing Your Board: A Step-by-Step Guide to Implementing Pol-*

icy Governance (Jossey-Bass, 1997), John Carver and Miriam Mayhew Carver, by ___(date)___ .

- Distribute The High-Performance Board Chapters Two, Three, and Four, and Resource B (Illustrative Policies) to all board members by no later than ___(date)___ .

- Have discussion of the "policy governance" approach at ___(date)___ board meeting; discuss, deliberate, and vote on whether to move forward with implementation.

- Assign follow-up and implementation planning to governance committee. Tasks include drafting a policy codification form, auditing board meeting minutes for the last three years to identify "implicit policies," and drafting an initial set of key policies for board discussion, deliberation, and vote.

- Conduct a workshop on crafting policies at board meeting by no later than ___(date)___; distribute CarverGuide 1: Basic Principles of Policy Governance to all board members.

Assign the responsibility of facilitating your board's principle-based approach to governing to a committee charged with drafting additional principles and bringing them to the full board for discussion, deliberation, and vote, and with preparing action plans for ensuring their effective implementation.

At least annually, assess whether your board is really governing on the basis of the principles it has adopted. In addition, note the extent to which each principle results in better performance and greater contributions. Do you have the principles you really need?

Parting Shots: The Conundrum of Change

You've probably seen it happen numerous times. A change initiative is introduced with considerable fanfare. It's a great idea and makes sense, but nonetheless it either fails to get off the ground or doesn't stick.

Deep Change: Barriers and Strategies

One of the best and most practical books we've read on this topic is *Leading Change* by John Kotter (Harvard Business School Press, 1996). He also wrote a companion article titled "Leading Change: Why Transformation Efforts Fail" (*Harvard Business Review,* March/April, 1995). We strongly recommend them.

Kotter argues that transformational efforts that seek to produce significant change fail because of eight common errors:

- Too much complacency
- Not creating a powerful guiding coalition
- Underestimating the need for a precise and empowering vision of what things could and should be like
- Dramatically undercommunicating the need for change and the vision
- Not removing obvious obstacles early in the process
- Not producing short-term wins
- Declaring victory too soon
- Neglecting to firmly anchor changes in the system's culture

He then presents sets of strategies for overcoming each of these barriers.

Inertia is a powerful force; all systems, including governance, are inherently change-resistant. In moving toward a principle-based approach, your board will be initiating very broad and deep change. Here are a few key concluding recommendations:

Secure the high ground first. The board chair and CEO must be committed to principle-based governance. Other members can serve as catalysts, but absent the full support of your board's leadership, it is highly unlikely that anything will happen. If you are the chair or CEO, you're on the way. If not, give them copies of this book, buy them dinner, start talking to begin building a cadre for mounting change.

Build consensus on the need for change—and don't start the transformation process until you have it. "Happy systems don't change." Your board must be dissatisfied with the status quo; it must also develop a vision of the way things could be at their very best. The difference between "is" and "could be" provides the motivation for change. Discussing the principles and practices introduced here, combined with a candid assessment of your board, is the point of departure.

Climb out of the routine trap. Most boards are mired in a cycle of activity where the routine overwhelms the nonroutine. Their time is limited and they spend so much of it actually governing that they have little energy left for improving how they govern. For your board to mount a transformation it must extricate itself from this trap. You'll have to step back from the routine, get out of the "way things have always been done" box, and find the time necessary to design and implement new systems and procedures. There are no easy paths here—but finding time to do the additional work of transformation is critical. Do an audit of your board's activities (in general, and particularly at its meetings). Identify things your board does that are irrelevant and inconsequential. Stop doing them and use the time to engineer governance improvement initiatives. We've found that scheduling a series of half-day mini-retreats over a year is one of the best ways to target a board's attention on developing, adopting, and implementing governing principles and best practices.

Be realistic. Transforming a board is like remodeling a house. It is a disruptive process requiring considerable effort; you will build some things that have to be rebuilt and encounter a number of difficulties along the way.

Expect conflict. Engaging in increasingly explicit and precise discussions about how your board should govern will raise issues that were not recognized or deliberately left fuzzy or even swept under the rug. Clarifying a problem always precipitates conflict regarding potential solutions. Such conflict (around ideas, rather than personalities) should be embraced as a way to build energy and stimulate creativity.

Celebrate initial victories. Change initiatives are sustained through a series of small wins. The recognition and celebration of short-term results provides evidence that the effort is worth it, undermines cynics and resisters, and builds motivation for the long run.

———————

There is a positive, systematic, and ongoing association between governance quality and organizational success. Your board can make a difference on behalf of stakeholders and add real value. Or it can rob the organization of its potential. Which type of board will yours be?

Resource A

The Sixty-Four Principles

1. The board realizes that it alone bears ultimate responsibility, authority, and accountability for the organization. It understands the importance of governance and undertakes its work with a sense of seriousness and purpose.

2. The board understands those factors that most affect governance quality and employs a coherent set of principles to govern.

3. The overarching obligation of a board is ensuring an organization's resources and capacities are deployed in ways that benefit its stakeholders. The board serves as their agent, representing, protecting, and advancing their interests and acting on their behalf.

4. The board identifies the organization's key stakeholders.

5. The board understands stakeholder interests and expectations.

6. The board decides and acts on behalf of stakeholders; it discharges its legal fiduciary duty of loyalty.

7. The board discharges its legal fiduciary duty of care.

8. The board understands the functions it must perform in order to meet its obligations.

9. The board understands and accepts its ultimate responsibility for determining the organization's ends and ensuring it has a plan for achieving them.

10. The board formulates the organization's vision.

11. The board specifies key organizational goals.

12. The board does not become directly involved in developing organizational strategies; it delegates this task to management.

13. The board understands it is ultimately responsible for ensuring high levels of executive performance.

14. The CEO is the board's only direct report.

15. When a vacancy occurs, the board selects the CEO.

16. The board has a CEO succession plan.

17. The board specifies its key expectations of the CEO.

18. Annually, employing explicit criteria, the board assesses the CEO's performance and contributions.

19. Annually, the board adjusts the CEO's compensation.

20. Should the need arise, the board is willing to terminate the CEO's employment.

21. The board understands that it is ultimately responsible for ensuring the quality of the organization's services or products.

22. The board has an explicit and precise working definition of quality.

23. The board develops a panel of quality indicators.

24. The board ensures the organization has a plan for improving quality.

25. The board understands it is ultimately responsible for the organization's financial health.

26. The board specifies key financial objectives for the organization.

27. The board ensures that management-devised budgets are aligned with financial objectives, key goals, and the vision.

28. The board develops a panel of financial indicators.

29. The board ensures that necessary financial controls are in place.

30. The board is ultimately responsible for itself—for its own performance and contributions.

31. The board understands that to govern effectively it must execute three core roles: policy formulation, decision making, and oversight.

32. The board formulates policies regarding its ultimate responsibilities.

33. The board makes decisions regarding matters requiring its attention and input.

34. The board oversees (monitors and assesses) key organizational processes and outcomes.

35. When it meets, the board spends the majority of its time performing its policy formulation, decision-making, and oversight roles.

36. The board acts only collectively; and once it does so, members support its policies and decisions.

37. The board has an explicit, precise, coherent, and empowering notion of the type of work it must do—its responsibilities and roles.

38. The board recognizes the importance of governance structure that is consciously designed based on explicit principles, criteria, and choices.

39. Governance structure is streamlined.

40. Unless there are extraordinarily compelling reasons to do otherwise, board size ranges from nine to nineteen members.

41. If governance structure is decentralized, the authority, responsibilities, and roles of parent and subsidiary boards are explicitly and precisely specified.

42. If advisory bodies are employed, their functions are clearly specified and differentiated from those of governing boards.

43. The board specifies the roles of committees and its relationship to them.

44. The number and type of committees are designed to reflect the board's responsibilities and facilitate and support its work.

45. The functions and tasks of committees are specified by the board and codified in a charter and work plan.

46. Governance structure is thoroughly assessed at regular intervals and modified if necessary.

47. The board proactively designs and manages its composition.

48. Members are recruited and selected on the basis of explicit criteria, employing a profiling process.

49. New board members participate in a carefully crafted and executed orientation process.

50. The board specifies member expectations.

51. The board has fixed term lengths and limits the number of terms members can serve.

52. The board periodically assesses the performance and contributions of every member; the results are employed to coach and develop members and make composition redesign decisions.

53. Board composition is nonrepresentational.

54. The CEO is a voting *ex officio* member of the board.

55. Insiders and those serving *ex officio* comprise less than 25 percent of the board's membership.

56. The board has its own budget.

57. The board has adequate staff support.

58. The board formulates annual objectives.

59. Meeting agendas are carefully devised plans for deploying the board's attention and time.

60. Board meetings are managed and conducted to promote high levels of effectiveness, efficiency, and creativity.

61. The chair is carefully selected, understands the role, and is able to perform it effectively.

62. The board is serious about continuous member development and has a plan for accomplishing it.

63. The board holds periodic retreats.

64. The board engages in a periodic self-assessment and formulates action plans to improve its performance and contributions.

Resource B

Illustrative Board Policies

Ends

• Strategies are management's means for accomplishing board-specified key goals and the vision. The task of devising organizational strategies is delegated to management. At least two months prior to the beginning of the fiscal year, management must submit its key strategies to the board (via its standing committee on ends). Each strategy must be explicitly linked to one or more board-formulated goals. Additionally, a rationale must be forwarded that denotes how pursuing the particular strategy will lead to accomplishing the goal or goals to which it is linked and to promoting realization of the vision.

Management

• The CEO is the agent of the board and its only direct report. The CEO is delegated full authority for conducting the organization's affairs, constrained only by the board's policies and decisions and subject to its oversight.
• The CEO is prohibited from authorizing, without prior board approval, individual capital expenditures exceeding $XXX,XXX; expenditures for improvement in facilities exceeding $XXX,XXX per project; leases exceeding $XXX,XXX in total value; expenditures for new programs or programmatic enhancements exceeding

$XXX,XXX per year; and contracts for the purchase of services exceeding $XXX,XXX.

Quality

• Management is directed to retain a consulting firm to conduct a periodic assessment (employing precise quantitative measures across multiple dimensions) of client satisfaction and the extent to which the organization's services and products meet client needs, and of employee satisfaction. Findings should be trended, compared to those of similar organizations, or benchmarked. Results of the assessment, in addition to management plans for correcting any deficiencies, should be presented to the board semiannually.

Finances

• The CEO is directed to design and implement, by no later than [date], a compliance program to ensure that violations of applicable law and regulations by the organization's employees and agents are prevented, detected, and reported and corrected. An annual audit should be conducted with a report forwarded to the board regarding how well the organization is complying with its legal and ethical obligations. This report should outline any recommended changes.

Structure, Composition, and Infrastructure

• Policies of the board regarding its functioning, structure, composition, and infrastructure can be found in the bylaws. These bylaws supersede all policies formulated by the board regarding its own activities.

• Members of the board appointed *ex officio* have the same agency and fiduciary duties as outside directors to represent the interests of the organization's stakeholders as a general class. That is, *ex officio* members are appointed to the board because they bring valuable expertise and perspectives; they are not appointed to represent the special interests of a particular stakeholder group.

• Each board member shall exercise good faith and best efforts in the performance of all governance obligations, responsibilities, and roles. Each board member will be held to a strict rule of loyalty, honesty, and fair dealing; no board member shall use a position on the board, or knowledge gained therefrom, in a manner that would create a material conflict of interest or the appearance of such. In all matters affecting the organization, each board member shall act exclusively on behalf of stakeholder interests. No board member shall accept any material compensation, gift, or other favor that could influence or appear to influence any actions or decisions in the performance of the board's role. Each member (by completing the board's annual conflict of interest questionnaire) shall disclose any employment, activity, investment, or other interests that might compromise or conflict with the interests of the organization and its stakeholders. Each board member shall immediately disclose to the chair potential material conflicts when they arise. Members shall not participate in any discussion, deliberation, or vote where they have a material conflict of interest. No member shall claim the status of an agent of the organization unless specifically authorized to do so by the board.

Resource C

Sample Committee Charters

Executive Committee

The executive committee acts for the full board in emergencies (where a quorum of the full board cannot be convened) and provides support to the chair in leading and planning the organization's governance. Its functions include:

- Developing, managing, and overseeing the board's budget

- Directing and overseeing staff assistance allocated to the board

- Providing advice and counsel to the board chair in appointing committee chairs and members

- Establishing ad hoc committees and appointing their members

- Drafting annual governance objectives and the work plan for board deliberation and approval

- Setting the agenda for each board meeting

- Reviewing and making recommendations to the board regarding removal of members in midterm

- Providing advice and counsel to the chair regarding ways to enhance board performance and contributions

- Serving as a sounding board for the CEO

- When the need arises, serving as the board's CEO search committee

- Undertaking other tasks as assigned by the board chair

Committee on Ends

The committee on ends assists the board in formulating policies, making decisions, and engaging in oversight that ensures that organizational ends (vision, goals, and strategies) advance and protect stakeholder interests. Its functions include:

- Helping the board to undertake a periodic analysis of key stakeholders including their interests, needs, and expectations

- Formulating or reformulating a draft organizational vision for board deliberation and action

- Formulating or reformulating draft organizational goals for board deliberation and action

- Engaging in a preliminary assessment of the extent to which annual management strategies are aligned with board-formulated vision and key goals and forwarding this assessment to the board for deliberation and action

- Recommending quantitative measures to be employed by the board in monitoring and assessing the extent to which the organization's vision is being fulfilled, goals are being accomplished, and key strategies are being effectively pursued

- Drafting policies regarding organizational ends and for-warding them to the board for deliberation and action

- Reviewing proposals regarding organizational ends sub-mitted by management and forwarding them (with commentary and recommendations) to the board for deliberation and action

- Preparing drafts of decisions regarding organizational ends that must be made by the board

- Undertaking an annual review and assessment of all board policies and decisions regarding organizational ends

- Performing other tasks dealing with organizational ends as assigned by the board

Committee on Executive Performance

The committee on executive performance assists the board in for-mulating policies, making decisions, and engaging in oversight to ensure high levels of executive performance. Its functions include:

- Conducting a review of the CEO succession plan and forwarding recommendations to the board regarding needed alterations at least every two years

- Working with the CEO to formulate annual personal performance expectations and forwarding them to the board for deliberation and approval

- On behalf of the board, undertaking an assessment of the CEO's performance; engaging in action planning with the CEO to improve performance; and forwarding this assessment and recommendations for adjustments in compensation to the board for deliberation and approval

- Conducting a review of the board's CEO assessment process every other year and making recommendations to the board for needed alterations in it

- Drafting policies regarding executive management performance and forwarding them to the board for deliberation and action

- Reviewing and analyzing proposals regarding executive management performance and forwarding them to the board for deliberation and action

- Drafting decisions regarding executive management performance that must be made by the board

- Recommending quantitative measures to be employed by the board in assessing the CEO's performance

- Undertaking an annual assessment of all board policies and decisions regarding CEO performance

- Performing other tasks related to the enhancement of executive management performance as assigned by the board

Quality Committee

The quality committee assists the board in formulating policies, making decisions, and engaging in oversight that ensures offering quality and client satisfaction. Its functions include:

- Working with management to undertake an annual analysis of client needs and forwarding this assessment to the board for its review

- Undertaking an annual assessment of the adequacy of the organization's quality and client satisfaction monitoring and management systems and forwarding recommendations to the board for its deliberation and action

- Drafting policies regarding offering quality and client satisfaction and forwarding them to the board for deliberation and action

- Reviewing management proposals regarding offering quality and client satisfaction and forwarding them to the board for deliberation and action

- Drafting decisions regarding offering quality and client satisfaction that must be made by the board

- Recommending quantitative measures to be employed by the board in assessing offering quality and client satisfaction

- Conducting a quarterly review of quality and satisfaction measures and forwarding an analysis to the board for deliberation and action

- Undertaking an annual assessment of all board policies and decisions regarding offering quality and client satisfaction

- Performing other tasks related to offering quality and client satisfaction as assigned by the board

Finance Committee

The finance committee assists the board in formulating policies, making decisions, and engaging in oversight that ensures the organization's financial health. Its functions include:

- Annually, forming a subcommittee to oversee the audit in addition to reviewing the auditor's opinion and management letter prior to deliberation and action by the board

- Reviewing all proposals from management regarding operational and capital expenditures that exceed board preapproved authorization limits and forwarding recommendations to the board for deliberation and action

- Annually, forwarding a memo to the board that reviews and assesses the overall financial health of the organization

- Serving as the point of first contact for the internal auditor's interaction with the board about any concerns the auditor raises regarding appropriate use and distribution of funds

- Drafting policies regarding finances and forwarding them to the board for deliberation and action

- Reviewing and analyzing proposals submitted by management regarding finances and forwarding them to the board for deliberation and action

- Drafting decisions regarding finances that must be made by the board

- Recommending quantitative measures to be employed by the board in assessing the organization's financial health

- Conducting a quarterly review of financial measures and forwarding an analysis to the board for deliberation and action

- Undertaking an annual assessment of all board policies and decisions regarding finances

- Performing other tasks related to the organization's financial health as assigned by the board

Governance Committee

The governance committee assists the board in improving its own functioning, structure, composition, and infrastructure. Its functions include:

- Directing and overseeing the assessment of the board, board committees, and individual board members every other year; reviewing such assessments; and making recommendations to the board regarding ways in which governance performance and contributions can be enhanced

- Planning the annual board retreat

- Directing and overseeing the board's continuing education and development activities

- Assessing the qualifications of individuals to assume board seats and forwarding nominations to the board

- Designing (and periodically assessing) the new board member orientation process

- Drafting policies regarding governance performance and forwarding them to the board for deliberation and action

- Drafting decisions regarding governance performance and forwarding them to the board for deliberation and action

- Recommending quantitative measures to be employed by the board in assessing governance performance and contributions

- Conducting an annual review of governance performance measures and forwarding an analysis to the board for deliberation and action

- Undertaking an annual assessment of all board policies and decisions regarding governance performance

- Performing other tasks related to governance performance as assigned by the board

Resource D

Illustrative Board Chair Position Description

The chair, working cooperatively with the CEO, provides leadership to the board. The chair also serves as symbol of the organization to both internal and external constituencies, and is an important member of the organization's leadership team.

Responsibilities

- Serving as a counselor and adviser to the CEO on matters of governance and board-executive relations

- Serving as the board's representative to key stakeholder groups

- Facilitating board meetings, ensuring they are focused, creative, effective, and efficient

- Serving as a mentor to other board members

- Serving as the board's exclusive contact with the media

- Serving as chair of the board's executive committee

- With advice of the executive committee, designating chairs of board committees

- Serving as an *ex officio* member of all board committees (although, except in the rarest instances, not expected to participate in their work and deliberations)

- With the assistance of the executive committee, drafting the board's annual objectives, developing the board's work plan, and formulating agendas for all board meetings

- Assuming other responsibilities and performing other tasks as directed by the board

Key Qualifications

- Have the time and energy to assume this demanding position, and agree to do so after careful self-assessment and reflection

- Have at least four years of experience as a member of this board

- Possess in-depth knowledge of the organization's challenges and opportunities, structure, functioning, and programs and services, and of its governance process

- Have been rated as "outstanding" on all board member performance evaluations for at least three years before assuming the office

- Have no general material conflicts of interest that would prohibit acting in the best interests of the organization and its stakeholders

- Be respected for personal and professional integrity, wisdom, intelligence, and judgment by the board and management team

- Have a collegial working relationship with the CEO

- Have a collegial working relationship with other board members

Term

The tenure of the board chair shall be a single two-year term. If an individual's term as chair exceeds the maximum board member term limit, that limit shall be extended by the number of years necessary for the individual to complete a full term as chair.

Nominations and Election

Nominees for the position of chair need not have been the board's vice chair or secretary; it is advisable (although not mandatory) that they have served at least one term on the board's executive committee. A special committee shall forward to the board one or more nominees for the position of chair. This committee shall be composed of the present board chair, the CEO, one at-large board member (elected by the full board), and one past chair who is not now sitting on the board (but who was elected by the full board).

Resource E

Illustrative Governance Principles

Our board governance practice is principle based. These principles are continuously and consistently applied to the way our board meets its obligations, fulfills its responsibilities, performs its roles, designs its structure, crafts its composition, and creates and maintains its infrastructure. These principles are thoroughly reviewed and if necessary modified annually.

- XYZ exists to benefit its stakeholders. Our board's purpose and overarching obligation is to ensure that stakeholder interests are protected and advanced, and that the organization's resources and capacities are effectively and efficiently deployed to do so.

  At least semiannually, our board will conduct a thorough stakeholder analysis, identifying key stakeholder groups and analyzing and understanding their needs and expectations.

  All issues that come before our board will be discussed, deliberated, and acted upon from a stakeholder perspective essential to meeting our legal fiduciary duty of loyalty.

- It is the duty of each board member to balance the needs and expectations of all stakeholders, not to advocate narrow interests or to represent specific interest groups.

- Our board formulates XYZ's vision on behalf of its stakeholders (and based on an analysis of their needs and expectations). The vision is an explicit, precise, fine-grained, and empowering image of what XYZ should become, in the future, at its very best; it denotes the organization's core purposes and values. The vision will be reviewed by our board and if necessary modified semiannually.

- Our board specifies XYZ's key goals, the most important things the organization must accomplish in order to fulfill the vision. Each year, our board will formulate, review, and if necessary modify these key goals. Employing explicit criteria, it will assess the extent they are being accomplished.

- Annually, our board specifies its most important performance expectations of the CEO.

- Employing explicit criteria and a formal process, the CEO's performance will be evaluated annually by our board on the basis of the extent to which stakeholder needs and expectations are being met; the vision is being fulfilled; key goals are being achieved; strategies are being effectively pursued; key financial performance and outcome objectives are being attained; and the CEO is achieving personal performance expectations.

- Employing explicit criteria and based on a valid methodology, the CEO will report to our board annually regarding quality of the organization's products and services and client satisfaction.

- Annually, our board will formulate a set of precise financial objectives for the organization.

- Each board committee will be required to develop annual objectives and a work plan. These plans will be reviewed and approved by the executive committee.

- Member service on our board will be limited to no more than three terms of three years each. The renewal of a member's term is not automatic, but rather based on an assessment of performance and contributions in addition to organizational and board needs.

- The performance and contribution of each board member will be assessed prior to the end of each term. This assessment will be employed by the executive committee to counsel the member regarding development and determine if the member should be renominated for an additional term.

- Each year, a set of governance goals will be developed; a specification of the most important things our board must accomplish. The degree to which these goals have been achieved will be assessed annually.

Resource F

For Further Reading

Books

Carver, J. *Boards That Make a Difference: A New Design for Leadership in Nonprofit and Public Organizations* (2nd ed.). San Francisco: Jossey-Bass, 1997.

Carver, J., and Carver, M. M. *Reinventing Your Board: A Step-by-Step Guide to Implementing Policy Governance.* San Francisco: Jossey-Bass, 1997.

Chait, R. P., and others. *The Effective Board of Trustees.* New York: Macmillan, 1991.

Houle, C. O. *Governing Boards: Their Nurture and Nature.* San Francisco: Jossey-Bass, 1989.

Pointer, D. D., and Orlikoff, J. E. *Board Work.* San Francisco: Jossey-Bass, 1999.

Articles

Chait, R. P., and Taylor, B. E. "Charting the Territory of Nonprofit Boards." *Harvard Business Review,* Jan. 1989.

Orlikoff, J. E. "Trouble in the Board Room: The Seven Deadly Sins of Ineffective Governance." *Healthcare Forum Journal,* May-June 1997.

Pointer, D. D., and Ewell, C. M. "Really Governing: What Type of Work Should Your Board Be Doing?" *Hospital and Health Services Administration,* May-June 1995.

Taylor, B. E., and others. "The New Work of the Nonprofit Board," *Harvard Business Review,* Sept.-Oct. 1996.

Web Sites

American Governance and Leadership Group
   http://www.americangovernance.com/
Board of Directors Network
   http://www.boarddirectorsnetwork.org/
Business Roundtable
   http://www.brtable.org/
California Public Employees Retirement System
   http://www.calpers-governance.org/
Conference Board
   http://www.conference-board.org/
Corporate Directors' Forum
   http://www.directorsforum.com/
Corporate Library
   http://www.thecorporatelibrary.net/
Encyclopedia of Corporate Governance
   http://www.encycogov.com/
Guide to Charitable Nonprofit Organizations
   http://nonprofit.about.com/
Internet Nonprofit Center
   http://www.nonprofits.org/
National Association of Corporate Directors
   http://www.nacdonline.org/
National Center for Nonprofit Boards
   http://www.boardsource.org/

Index